A BIRDER'S GUIDE
TO TRINIDAD AND TOBAGO
by William L. Murphy
1995

Scarlet Ibis by Pat Moore

Cover: Tufted Coquette by Peter LaTourette
at the Asa Wright Nature Center.

Published by
Peregrine Enterprises, Inc.
1011 Ann Street
Parkersburg, West Virginia 26101
murph3000@aol.com

First edition November 1986
Second edition December 1995

Library of Congress Cataloging-in-Publication Data

Murphy, William L., 1950-
  A birder's guide to Trinidad and Tobago / by William L.
Murphy. -- 2nd ed.
vi + 160 p. 14 x 17 cm.
  Includes index.
  ISBN 0-941475-02-6 (alk. paper)
  1. Bird watching--Trinidad and Tobago-Guidebooks. 2.
  Trinidad and Tobago--Guidebooks. I. Title.
QL681.T7M87 1995
598'. 0723472983--dc20

Peregrine Enterprises, Inc.
1011 Ann Street, Parkersburg, West Virginia, USA 26101
murph3000@aol.com

Printed in the United States of America

TABLE OF CONTENTS

Wetlands

Golden-headed manakin, by Don R. Eckelberry

FOREWORD

A Birder's Guide to Trinidad and Tobago is a welcome addition to the limited documentation available on any aspect of the rich natural heritage of Trinidad and Tobago. It provides excellent guidelines for finding places where the varied birdlife of both islands is most likely to be seen.

This book can be a valuable companion for any birder, inexperienced or experienced, who wishes to observe and document as many species as possible in a short space of time. Its pleasant conversational style, candid descriptions, firsthand information regarding transportation, accommodations, costs, etc., and accurate details for finding one's way around as an individual, make this book useful not only to visiting birders but also to nature buffs and other visitors seeking a tropical experience.

Indeed, this book is an excellent introduction for the layperson with no prior interest in birds. The enthusiastic descriptions of the abundance of birdlife that can be seen in easily accessible, "run of the mill" places can spark the interest and imagination of even the most disinterested non-birder, whether visiting or residing in Trinidad and Tobago.

The useful layout of sections for quick reference and especially the inclusion of bar graphs of the seasonal occurrence of bird species will enable birders with special interests to plan visits for times of year when particular species are most abundant, or to concentrate only on areas where such birds are likely to occur. Thus, this book can be used by visiting researchers and amateurs alike as a valuable planning guide.

It is hoped that *A Birder's Guide to Trinidad and Tobago* will serve not only to increase interest in birding among citizens of our country and visitors alike, but that it will also stimulate birders to pursue their birding activities carefully, enabling future generations to enjoy similar pleasures.

Carol J James

Dr. Carol James
Head, Wildlife Section
Forestry Division
Ministry of Agriculture, Lands & Food Production
Trinidad and Tobago

PREFACE

The names Trinidad and Tobago have an almost magical appeal to birders worldwide. The accessibility and affordability of trips to these islands, in addition to the magnificent birds they host, make them ideal places for birders to visit. Virtually everyone speaks English, customs are familiar ones, and the ambiance is one of gaiety and friendliness.

Of all the Caribbean islands, Trinidad is the most bountifully blessed with birdlife. Nearly 400 species have been recorded, a number astonishing to birders familiar with the rather ornithologically depauperate Caribbean islands to the north. The majority of species known to have occurred on either island are admirably described and illustrated in Richard ffrench's masterful *A Guide to the Birds of Trinidad and Tobago*; the publication you now hold is meant to be used in conjunction with ffrench's guide. Through these pages I hope to encourage you to see for yourself the engaging birds of Trinidad and Tobago and to experience, as I have, their singular beauty.

The secret of Trinidad's wealth of species results in part from its great variety of habitats, which range from open ocean to tall mountains and from scrub-covered deserts to emerald rainforests. An abundance of perennially available fruits and seeds provides forage for resident species and for migrants from both North and South America.

Trinidad and Tobago use the metric system; therefore, measurements in this guide are given in metric units with English-system measurements provided in some instances for purposes of comparison and to help you avoid endless conversions. Likewise, the cost of some items and services are also given in both Trinidad and Tobago dollars and U.S. dollars, the latter usually rounded to the next whole dollar. All prices mentioned in this publication are subject to change, of course.

I'd greatly appreciate receiving any additional information on locations or of sightings of birds in Trinidad and Tobago. Such information would be very helpful in future editions of this guide. Address all correspondence to 1011 Ann Street, Parkersburg, West Virginia, USA 26101 or on the Internet at murph3000@aol.com.

ACKNOWLEDGMENTS

This book is dedicated to Dr. Donald H. Messersmith (president of World Nature Tours, Inc., P.O. Box 693, Woodmoor Station, Silver Spring, Maryland, USA 20901), a superb educator and dear friend to whom I owe my love of the birds of Trinidad and Tobago. By instructing me in ornithology and entomology, training me as a bird tour guide, and later hiring me as tour escort on my first trip to Trinidad, he enabled me to experience a tropical blend of birdlife that has since become an obsession with me and which has resulted in many return visits to the islands — and in the production of this guide.

Among the many other people I would like to thank for their inspiration and help are my wife, Mary Lou, my parents, Bernadette and Lawrence Murphy, the late Manny Arias, Barry Cooper, Paul DuMont, Mary Gustafson, Dave Hardy, Gail Mackiernan, Walter Marcisz, Winston Nanan, Frank Nicoletti, Phil Olsen, Jogie Ramlal, Chandler Robbins, and Claudia Wilds. My brother Jim accompanied me during my most productive period in Trinidad, and my brother Joe facilitated the layout and publication of this book. Rob Gibbs and William C. Young in particular have been very helpful during my explorations of the area covered by this guide. Dr. Carol James and her staff of the Wildlife Section, Forestry Division, Ministry of Agriculture, Lands & Food Production of Trinidad and Tobago have contri-buted valuable information on the distribution of birdlife in the islands. Dr. James also provided an exceptionally careful review of the manuscript. Always charming and helpful, and especially deserving of my thanks, are Mrs. Victoria Soo Poy and Mr. Eric Patience, former managers of the Mount St. Benedict Guest House and Asa Wright Nature Center, respectively. Margaret Schaeffer, manager of Caligo Ventures, provided information on the Asa Wright Nature Center and biology programs currently offered there.

Special thanks are due to the late Robert and to Mark Garland for the use of their darkroom, to Steve and Diane Rose for the use of their recordings of bird songs, to Jesse Brandon for the use of state-of-the-art recording equipment, to Pat Moore for producing the original cover of this guide, to Brent B. Nelson of Graphic Interface, Beltsville, Maryland, for designing the cover, to Don R. Eckelberry for the use of his illustrations, and to Jeanne Gildersleeve for her expertise at making this book aesthetically pleasing.

Parkersburg, West Virginia USA
December 20, 1995

HOW TO USE THIS BOOK

I wrote this guide to allow birders from all parts of the world to learn about Trinidad and Tobago, to make arrangements to visit the islands, and to enjoy the birds found there. I assume that you'll be at least slightly familiar with the geography of the islands and carry a road map, or that you'll be affiliated with a tour group. In any event, before visiting an area yourself or on a scheduled field trip, be sure to read the appropriate sections of this guide in advance. Then refer to the section on specialties for information about the particular species of birds you're likely to see. With the exception of Little Tobago Island, the coverage of this book doesn't extend to offshore islands such as Soldado Rock, Chacachacare, Monos, St. Giles Island, etc.

In other parts of this guide I've provided information to allow you to direct your attention either toward finding a large number of species of birds or toward concentrating on finding particular species of interest. The sections on locations provide details about getting to and birding in particular areas, whereas the section on specialties provides details about individual species. Finally, the bar graph section provides visual information concerning the relative abundance of species throughout the year.

Distances are shown in kilometers. Unless otherwise stated, these distances represent the interval from the last place mentioned, not from the starting point. Odometer readings vary from vehicle to vehicle; test the calibration of the odometer in your rental car by comparing the distances between two landmarks to those provided here, then adjust your readings accordingly on your excursions.

Birders can readily find most species in Trinidad and Tobago by visiting the proper habitat during the proper season and by observing the birdlife for a few hours. Other species, even some permanent residents, you'll find only with great difficulty. If you wish to see the greatest number of species, visit as many different habitats as you can. If you wish to concentrate on seeing a few species of special interest to you, then read the section on specialties and visit the places suggested. Even if you're trying to amass a long list, by approximately the fifth day of birding you should've seen a great many species and likely will be ready for some specialized birding. To increase your chances of seeing the rarities, follow the example of Paul DuMont, one of North America's top rarity locators, and look at every bird — twice.

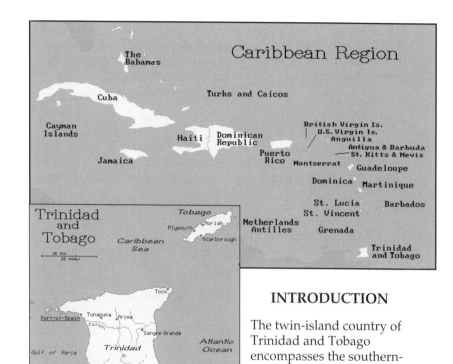

Caribbean Region

The Bahamas

Cuba

Turks and Caicos

Cayman Islands

Haiti

Dominican Republic

Jamaica

Puerto Rico

British Virgin Is.
U.S. Virgin Is.
Anguilla
Antigua & Barbuda
St. Kitts & Nevis
Montserrat
Guadeloupe
Dominica
Martinique
St. Lucia
St. Vincent
Barbados
Grenada

Netherlands Antilles

Trinidad and Tobago

Tobago

Moriah

Plymouth

Scarborough

Caribbean Sea

25 Km
15 miles

Toco

Port-of-Spain

Tunapuna

Arima

Caroni

Sangre Grande

Gulf of Paria

Trinidad

Atlantic Ocean

San Fernando

Rio Claro

Princes Town

Moruga

Pierreville

Debe

Siparia

Guayaguayare

INTRODUCTION

The twin-island country of Trinidad and Tobago encompasses the southern-most pair of islands in the Caribbean chain, small chips of South America that lie just off the coast of Venezuela, only about 10° north of the Equator. The southern coast of Trinidad lies just 12km north of the mainland of South America, across from the delta of the Orinoco River. Tobago lies 34km north-east of Trinidad.

Visitors almost universally proclaim the climate on both islands to be ideal, especially in the mountains. On the whole, temperatures average 29°C. (84°F.) during the day and 23°C. (74°F.) at night. The national language is English. The human population is about 1.3 million (1995). Many forms of transportation are available, and all are reliable. Electricity is 110 and 220 volts, 60 cycles. Trinidad and Tobago operate year-round on Eastern Standard Time, four hours behind Greenwich Mean Time.

The two islands of Trinidad and Tobago are only distantly related to each other biologically and geologically. Trinidad was formed in the same series of geological events that shaped the rest of the South American mainland. To that initial body the Orinoco River added considerable sedimentary contributions. The formation of the Northern Range finished the picture, consisting of scrapings from a tectonic plate being subsumed beneath the one on which Trinidad rests. This process continues today and is the source of the seismic activity in the area, along with such phenomena as geothermal vents and mud volcanos.

Trinidad broke off formal geological relations with the mainland about 10,000 years ago, at the end of an Ice Age during which much of the earth's seawater was tied up in the ice caps. Water from the melting ice drowned all but the mountain peaks on the land bridge that connected Trinidad with Venezuela. The flora and fauna of Trinidad thus became isolated from that of the mainland.

In contrast, Tobago rests on an eastward-moving tectonic plate that once was adjacent to the Lake Maracaibo region of western Venezuela. Even today the flora, fauna, and geology of Tobago are much more closely allied with those of western Venezuela than they are with those of its contemporary neighbor, Trinidad. During one of my early visits to Tobago I collected several specimens of what has turned out to be the only species of snail-killing fly on that island. In support of the theory that Tobago originated far west of its present location, the next easternmost location of the fly species is some 600 miles west, near Lake Maracaibo.

Because of the proximity of Trinidad and Tobago to South America, the fauna of both islands is far richer than that of any other West Indian island. In addition, the great diversity of habitats offers opportunities for selective birdwatching and makes the country as a whole a veritable paradise for birders and other naturalists. A plethora of feeding, staging, and nesting areas are available to suit the needs of even those species of birds that require unique and rare ecological niches. Readily accessible habitats include elfin forest, montane rainforest, lowland rainforest, savannah grassland, freshwater swamp, saltwater swamp, freshwater reservoir, ocean beach, and open ocean, as well as a wide variety of cultivated areas and formerly cultivated areas that are regenerating naturally. To birders, the unusually easy access to many of the bird-rich habitats and the occurrence of a manageable number of bird species help enhance the already powerful attraction of Trinidad and Tobago.

GEOGRAPHY

Trinidad is somewhat rectangular in shape, 80km by 60km, and is essentially level except for three east-to-west mountain ranges. The Northern Range, which is really the easternmost spur of the Andes, averages the highest of the three ranges, with El Cerro del Aripo and El Tucuche rising to over 940m. Much of the Northern Range is covered with lush rainforest and coffee-cocoa-citrus plantations, either active or abandoned. The eastern third of the Northern Range is very sparsely populated and contains pristine rainforest. The Northern Range receives more rainfall than any other part of Trinidad, as humid air from the Atlantic rises over the peaks, cools, and releases its moisture. In the wettest areas, rainfall may reach 500cm (200 inches) per year, but elsewhere rainfall rarely exceeds 200cm (80 inches) per year. A chain of arid islands dots the channel ("The Dragon's Mouth") that lies between the western tip of northern Trinidad near Chaguaramas and the tip of the Paria Peninsula of Venezuela.

Trinidad's Central Range stretches diagonally from the Gulf of Paria in the west across central Trinidad and northeastward to the Atlantic Ocean, reaching a maximum elevation of 307m on Mount Tamana. To the south are forests, swamps, private oil fields, and the bituminous Pitch Lake. In the southeastern corner are the 250-m-high Trinity Hills, from which Columbus derived the island's name.

The remaining areas of Trinidad are mainly lowlands that are, or were, almost entirely cultivated, except for the North Oropuche and Nariva Swamps in the east and the Caroni, South Oropuche, and Icacos Swamps in the west and southwest. Trinidad's shorelines range from palm-fringed sandy beaches to vertical rock cliffs.

Tobago is shaped like a northeastward-pointing fish. Its overall topography is more rugged than that of Trinidad, but the mountains aren't so high; the highest point, Pigeon Peak, reaches only 576m. Partly because of a lack of high peaks or ridges to deflect moist breezes upwards, Tobago is drier overall than is Trinidad. Rainforests cover most of the mountainous spine that runs about two-thirds the length of the island. The southernmost area (the "tail" of the "fish") consists of highly fertile flatlands and is home to the majority of Tobagonians. Here, too, are found the only extensive wetlands on Tobago. Like the coastline of Trinidad, that of Tobago is diverse, being sandy in some stretches and rocky in others. St. Giles Island and Little Tobago Island, both of which lie off Tobago's northern coast, harbor nesting seabirds.

NATURAL HISTORY

That the fauna and flora of Trinidad and Tobago resemble those of nearby Venezuela in composition is partly a result of the islands' continental origin and proximity to South America. The list of species is impressive, with records of 108 species of mammals, 55 reptiles, 25 amphibians, and 617 butterflies. Similar diversity is found in many other less conspicuous animal groups and among the tropical plants, many of which are endemic to Trinidad or Tobago. Birders have recorded more than 430 species of birds, of which about 250 are known to breed, yet the number of species of birds isn't overwhelming to the visitor from abroad. Indeed, a trip to Trinidad and Tobago offers one of the finest introductions to birding in the tropics. No other area in the West Indies — indeed few areas of comparable size elsewhere in tropical America — can match this species diversity.

On excursions to Trinidad and Tobago, it's commonplace for birders to add 120 species to their life lists during a 7-day stay, with another 15-20 additional species possible with even a single day's visit to Tobago. As an added bonus, birders can observe migrant species of South American origin on both islands during the Northern Hemisphere's summer months. Persons venturing no farther afield than the veranda ("gallery") of one of the guest houses have tallied lists totaling 40-60 species observed in a day.

Although no club exists in Trinidad and Tobago for the study of birds exclusively, the **Trinidad and Tobago Field Naturalists' Club** serves to bring together all persons interested in the study of natural history, the diffusion of the knowledge of natural history, and the conservation of nature. The Club has been in existence for more than 100 years, having been founded in 1891. Monthly lecture meetings are held at St. Mary's College in Port-of-Spain early in the evening of the second Thursday of each month and are well worth attending. Field excursions are conducted on the last Sunday of each month except December. Membership in the Club is open to all persons of at least fifteen years of age who subscribe to the objectives of the club. You can obtain additional information from the Honorable Secretary, Box 642, Port-of-Spain, Trinidad, W.I.

The newly formed **Trinidad and Tobago Bird Records Committee** is the official organization to which you should submit documentation of unusual species. Photographs are most desirable, but comprehensive written notes are welcome, especially those made in the field before you consult any field guides. Please include the following information with your submission: date, time, location (as specifically as possible), observer(s) name(s), address(es), details of the sighting including length of time and distance from bird(s), lighting conditions, optical equipment used, and observer(s) familiarity with the species and with similar species. Include anything and everything you saw, heard, and remember. Often details that observers note but which *do not appear* in field guides are familiar to the committee members and enable them to reach a decision to accept an otherwise borderline submission.

For the sake of simplicity, please submit your records either to the manager of the Asa Wright Nature Center, who will forward them to the current president of the committee, or to me, a current member of the committee. When my term expires, I'll continue to forward submissions to the current president.

CLIMATE, CLOTHING, AND EQUIPMENT

Exceptionally fine birding is possible in Trinidad and Tobago every month of the year. Because the climate is so constant, it's easy to pack the right clothes for a visit. I always recommend that birders wear a hat on sunny days. If you don't, and if you get light-headed, headachy, and nauseated from sunstroke, it won't matter whether or not you're wearing Rockport hiking shoes or not; you're outta there! Keeping the midday sun off your head will allow you to continue birding at times when the hatless will retreat into the protective shade.

Wearing lightweight clothes is a good plan in all seasons, with a light jacket or sweater for the cool nights, especially at higher elevations. Persons sensitive to sunlight will find a long-sleeved blouse or shirt to be indispensable. A wide-brimmed hat is recommended for protection against sun and rain. Long slacks or light-weight denim jeans are advisable, especially if you anticipate exploring savannahs covered with razor grass, but you'll find that short pants are comfortable to wear in most areas. Rain gear, such as a pocket poncho with a hood, is recommended during the rainy season if you plan to spend time away from shelter, but if you're caught in a shower you'll find that the rain is warm and pleasant unless torrential, and you'll dry quickly enough. Dress casually but neatly at all times unless you're advised otherwise. Bring swimwear if you wish to enjoy the abundant beaches, rivers, and swimming pools, and by all means if you plan to visit Tobago, where the coral reefs are among the world's best for snorkeling. Note that swimwear is inappropriate for casual wear in most establishments.

Tennis shoes ("sneakers") are the footwear of choice on most outings; consider bringing an extra pair to use when your wet pair is drying or to wear as foot protection while snorkeling. Hiking shoes are very worthwhile on some of the more arduous mountain trails, especially under muddy conditions.

Other useful items to bring include extra batteries, alarm clock, notebook and mechanical pencil (not a pen because ink runs when wet) for recording observations, daypack, polarizing sunglasses, portable tape recorder, and plastic zip-locking bags to protect items from dust, moisture, sea air, and ants. I've found that dental floss or dental tape can be a real godsend to have after I've enjoyed a stringy mango. Sunscreen lotion is essential even if you're not sensitive to the sun. Make sure that your sunscreen contains at least 5% PABA or it will be ineffective against the strong tropical sunlight. A telescope and tripod are very useful, especially when you're birding along the coast or in a swamp. Especially useful are mirror-lens telescopes with their great light-gathering ability; their use allows identification of backlighted birds in the forest canopy that otherwise might be virtually unidentifiable. You may find a video camera useful for recording your experiences. You may wish to bring a flashlight for nocturnal prowls, along with a more powerful spotlight for sighting nocturnal birds; extremely bright battery-powered spotlights are available at ever-decreasing prices. Finally, don't forget to pack the essentials — binoculars, camera, lenses, film, Richard ffrench's *A Guide to the Birds of Trinidad and Tobago*, and this book.

MAPS

The Lands and Surveys Office in Port-of-Spain sells detailed road and topographic maps at reasonable prices. The office is located at 18 Abercromby Street, near the government's Red House and across the street from the *Trinidad Guardian* newspaper office and NBS radio. Office hours are 8:00 a.m. to noon and 1:00 p.m. to 2:45 p.m., Monday through Friday. Their telephone number is (809) 624-8023.

A comprehensive road map of Trinidad (Edition 4, Mapping & Control Section of the Lands & Surveys Division, Ministry of Agriculture, Lands & Food Production) is available for TT$10 from the Lands and Surveys Office. Road maps of Tobago are produced in lesser quantities than their Trinidad counterparts and thus are frequently out of stock, but when available you may purchase them for about the same price as the road map of Trinidad. Topographic maps (1:10,000 scale) are available for TT$4. Particularly useful topographic map sections include Sheet 24, covering the Tunapuna-Arima-Piarco quadrant and Sheet 14, covering the quadrant north of Tunapuna-Arima and including parts of the Northern Range and Blanchisseuse Road. Both maps are in Series E 804 (D.O.S. 316/1). You can obtain maps in advance by mail or in person on weekdays except for holidays. Travel bookstores in some of the larger cities in North America and Europe also carry maps of Trinidad, and a few carry maps of Tobago. If you rent a car, be sure to ask for a road map.

RECOMMENDED BOOKS AND TAPE

Most birders initially are surprised to learn that James Bond's *Birds of the West Indies* excludes Trinidad from its geographic coverage. Bond and most other ornithologists correctly place Trinidad in the South American faunal zone, which is radically different from the West Indies in avian distribution.

Instead of Bond's book, obtain a copy of the second edition (1992) of *A Guide to the Birds of Trinidad and Tobago*, by Richard ffrench. I consider this book an essential companion on birding trips to Trinidad and Tobago. ffrench provides the reader with information on habitat and status, range and subspecies, banding status, appearance, measurements, voice, food, and behavior. Be sure to read the introduction to this wonderful book, which consists of adetaileddescription of the geography and natural history of the islands.

If you consider yourself to be a serious birder, you'd be wise to bring field guides covering possible extralimital species. In particular, De Schauensee & Phelps' *Guide to Birds of Venezuela* is most useful for identifying South American species, especially flycatchers and raptors, and may be used in place of ffrench's guide in a pinch; the greatest drawback to the exclusive use of De Schauensee & Phelps' book in Trinidad and Tobago is the large number of birds illustrated therein that rarely if ever occur in Trinidad and Tobago. Because increasing numbers of extralimital strays are being reported on both islands, birders also may wish to pack a copy of Heinzel *et al.*'s *The Birds of Britain and Europe* and the National Geographic Society's *Field Guide to the Birds of North America*, second edition (1987).

For a detailed examination of the human history of Trinidad and Tobago, the standard work is Eric Williams' *History of the People of Trinidad and Tobago* (André Deutsch Ltd., 105 Great Russell St., London WC1, United Kingdom).

A **cassette recording** of 39 species of birds from Trinidad and Tobago is available for US$10 (postage and handling included) from the author (1011 Ann Street, Parkersburg, West Virginia 26101 USA). The arrangement of songs on the tape is consistent with that in the latest *Check-List of the American Ornithologists Union* (AOU). Included are southern lapwing, pale-vented pigeon, orange-winged parrot, smooth-billed ani, ferruginous pygmy-owl, green hermit, white-tailed and collared trogons, blue-crowned motmot, channel-billed toucan, pale-breasted and stripe-breasted spinetails, gray-throated leaftosser, black-crested and barred antshrikes, white-fringed antwren, silvered antbird, black-faced antthrush, tropical pewee, great kiskadee, fuscous and boat-billed flycatchers, gray kingbird, bearded bellbird, white-bearded and blue-backed manakins, long-billed gnatwren, cocoa and white-necked thrushes, tropical mockingbird, scrub greenlet, rufous-browed peppershrike, tropical parula, bananaquit, silver-beaked tanager, blue-black grassquit, yellow-hooded blackbird, carib grackle, and crested oropendola.

By listening to this tape several times before visiting Trinidad and Tobago, you'll find yourself familiar with many of the bird songs of the islands.

Available from Nina Steffee at the following address are ffrench's guide and many other hard-to-find natural history materials.

Address –   Russ's Natural History Books
             P.O. Box 1089
             Lake Helen, Florida 32744-1089 USA
             (904) 228-3356

PERSONAL COMFORT, HEALTH, AND SAFETY

No inoculations, vaccinations, or anti-malarial pills are required for a visit to Trinidad and Tobago, but the cautious visitor should obtain a yellow fever vaccination. Yellow fever is transmitted by certain forest-inhabiting mosquitoes to which the average visitor will never be exposed, but intrepid birders often penetrate remote forests inhabited by red howler and other species of monkeys that serve as vectors of the yellow fever virus.

The drinking water on both islands is safe and need not be boiled or otherwise treated before use. If you'd rather not try the local water, you'll be able to quench your thirst with an abundance of fresh-squeezed fruit juice and other beverages, especially soft drinks, coffee, and tea. Vegetables and fresh fruits, when eaten in reasonable quantities, don't seem to induce the intestinal disorders usually so common among travelers to the tropics.

Pest insects, primarily horseflies, sand flies, and mosquitoes, are rarely a problem except at certain periods during the rainy season. At those times you'll find insect repellent and anti-itch creams to be useful. Most biting insects are easily repelled by any of the commercially available preparations. Chiggers (which are actually mites, not insects) can be common during the dry season, but you can successfully avoid their bites by liberal and frequent applica-

8

tion of insect repellent spray to your shoes or sneakers and to the lower parts of your slacks or legs. Contrary to the popular belief that a chigger burrows into the skin, it's long gone by the time the itching begins. When feeding, a chigger inserts a tube through the skin and injects a proteinaceous anticoagulant, which causes a localized allergic reaction that manifests itself several hours later,  long after the chigger has dropped off. If you do get a chigger bite or two, any anaesthetizing sunburn preparation will numb the itch for hours.

Only four species of poisonous snakes are known from Trinidad — the bushmaster, the fer-de-lance, and two small coral snakes. Snake bites are very rare, and fatalities are almost unknown. Most deaths by snakebite are of children who've been bitten by one of the coral snakes, the bites of which aren't unusually painful. The bite goes unreported and untreated, and the child dies of respiratory failure a few days later. If you spot a snake, avoidance is the best course of action to follow. No poisonous snakes are known to occur on Tobago.

Reluctant though I am to add a somber note to this book, there is no way to avoid discussing crime these days. As is now true in most other countries, in Trinidad and Tobago the greatest threat to personal safety may well be from your fellow man. The population of Trinidad has exploded in recent years, along with that of Tobago, although the latter to a much lesser extent; Tobago is still almost crime-free. Concurrently the crime rate on Trinidad has jumped alarmingly. Initially the increase resulted mostly from property crimes, such as theft and burglary, which stemmed from the abject poverty of some of the illegal immigrants. Unfortunately, many crimes are now of the violent sort, including kidnaping, rape, and murder. Drug trafficking accounts for most of the violence and is concentrated in heavily populated areas, especially Port-of-Spain. (Although no cause-and-effect relationship is known, it's interesting to note that the crime rate has risen in conjunction with the increase in violent American cable TV programs shown in Trinidad and Tobago.) Whatever the reason for the increased violence, crime must now be taken seriously whereas in prior decades it wasn't a concern except perhaps in Port-of-Spain. Visitors frequently are targeted because they are easily discerned in crowds and because they often conspicuously display trappings of wealth (binoculars, cameras, video cameras, etc.). Most large properties now employ security services, at least at night, for the safety of their guests and that of the buildings and their contents.

Moreover, because we birders with our expensive optical equipment often are the ultimate in conspicuous wealth, we must be extremely cautious on excursions. For example, since 1990 I've felt uncomfortable without an armed guard when venturing with birding groups into one of Trinidad's most productive birding areas, the Port-of-Spain sewage lagoons. The proximity of the lagoons to the shanty town along the Beetham Highway, home mainly to impoverished immigrants from South America, has compelled many bird tour companies to delete the Port-of-Spain lagoons from their itineraries. Visiting birders most often are robbed when traveling alone, but occasional reports surface of entire birding groups being robbed at gunpoint.

At this point let me hasten to add that I've never experienced any crime at all on any of the 35+ tours I've led to Trinidad and Tobago nor on any of the numerous reconnoitering visits I've made over the years. On those occasions when I've encountered other people when far afield and remote from habitation, I've always taken the initiative of holding up my binoculars, pointing in the general direction of the nearby birds, then extending my open right hand while smiling and saying, quite loudly, "Respect!" As a universal gesture of good will, perhaps it may be corny, but so far, so good. (I have a recurring dream of such an encounter, wherein I have the opportunity to use a line from the movie *Bill and Ted's Excellent Adventure* — "I'm totally weak, and I can't fight at all!")

To reduce your chances of becoming a victim of crime in Trinidad and Tobago, you must behave as you would in any major city. Entrust all jewelry (including wedding rings), cash, travelers' checks, and other portable valuables to the hotel manager, where they will be locked in a safe. Likewise entrust your passport and airline tickets to the hotel. Keep your room locked at all times, and if possible, verify the identity of anyone who knocks on your door before you unlock it. When on field trips, present a subdued appearance. If you must carry cash, carry it in a hidden pouch or money belt. Don't drape yourself in optical equipment so as to resemble a walking Nikon advertisement. Don't bird alone, except on guarded nature reserves such as at the Asa Wright Nature Center or the Pointe-à-Pierre Wild Fowl Trust. Avoid Port-of-Spain and Wallerfield at night in particular; the latter site is a notorious drug dealing site. If you drive, don't pick up strangers. Wherever possible, stay close to your group.

Just a few words about sex. It's just as popular in Trinidad and Tobago as it is elsewhere, and many advertisements contain broad sexual overtones that some visitors find offensive. AIDS is present in epidemic proportions in relation to its frequency in the U.S. or Great Britain. If you're female, you should be aware that the notorious tropical macho tendencies reach their zenith in Trinidad and Tobago. Men may leer at you, shout compliments at you, whistle and make other less identifiable sounds at you, and perhaps even make overt suggestions as how you might spend some of your vacation time in a clearly non-birding mode. Much to the consternation of tour companies such as mine, even the local guides have been known to press ardent advances on a woman or women in a tour group. If such attention is to your liking, "No problem, mon!" If not, you may do well to ignore it the first time and hope that it was an isolated event. If the behavior recurs, then while the words of love and lust still linger in the air, tell him forcefully that you dislike that kind of attention and that you'll find any further such attention from him to be insulting.

MONEY

The unit of exchange in Trinidad and Tobago is the TT dollar (henceforth TT$, pronounced "tee-tee"), which is valued on a floating exchange rate. As of this writing (late 1995) the exchange rate is US $1.00 to TT $5.50. Your hometown bank should be able to quote you the current exchange rate. When spending foreign currency in Trinidad and Tobago, be sure to insist on the full exchange rate at hotels and stores; cashiers often will use a lower rate, so beware. Upon your arrival at Piarco Airport, you may be approached by black-market dealers offering half again as much as the current exchange rate for your national currency. Before jumping for this rate, consider that local banks later won't exchange your unspent TT$ for your national currency unless you have a bank receipt for at least the amount you wish to redeem. You may find yourself flying home with an attractive but unspendable wad of TT$ that your bank may not wish to redeem. The banks at Piarco Airport offer a competitive exchange rate, and they will provide you with the all-important receipt. It's prudent to play it safe and legal by using the services of a bank if you need to exchange your currency. An exception to the above

11

caution pertains to the exchange of small sums (US$100 or less) by guides, hotel managers, etc., who often have a genuine need for US$ and are more than happy to provide you with a fair exchange rate.

That having been said, rest assured that the currency preferred throughout the islands is the American dollar.

WHEN TO VISIT

It's possible for even a novice birder to list 130-225 species of birds in Trinidad and Tobago in two weeks during any month of the year. North American migrants are most abundant from October to March, and South American migrants are most abundant from May to September. Consult the bar graph section of this book for information on the seasonal abundance of individual species.

The traditional time to visit Trinidad and Tobago formerly was January through March, coincident with the driest time of the year. During February the islands pulsate day and night to the sound of steel drums as the annual holiday of Carnival is celebrated. At this time many prices are inflated, especially the price of accommodations and transportation, including jet fares. In recent years tour groups have begun visiting the islands throughout the year.

Trinidad and Tobago experience a rainy season between late May and September and another between October and December; September often is a dry month. Even during the rainy season rain doesn't fall continuously. Torrential downpours are the rule, with intense shower activity almost every day, mostly brief and mainly in the early afternoon. Birding isn't so negatively affected as might be imagined, though. Many species forage frantically between showers and are thus even more conspicuous than they are during the drier times of the year. Moreover, the rainy season coincides with the Southern Hemisphere's winter and is thus the only time to observe South American species that visit Trinidad and Tobago during the southern winter.

Some advantages of visiting during the rainy season include vast reductions in airfares and prices of hotels and guest houses; a virtual lack of other tourists; assured availability of accommodations, rental cars, guides, and seating on air shuttles to Tobago; fewer chiggers; and the presence of South American migrant species. Disadvantages include the emergence of mosquitoes, the need to carry an umbrella or stay near shelter, and an abundance of muddy trails and back roads.

Pesonally speaking, I've conducted birding tours to Trinidad and Tobago during all months of the year. My favorite month to visit is June, when sea turtles and seabirds are nesting and South American migrants are present. On the downside, it often rains once or twice daily. My least favorite time to visit (the only one, actually) is during the first half of May, at the tail end of the dry season, when much of the vegetation is sere and parched and the air is hazy with pink dust blown across the Atlantic from the Sahara Desert.

In my estimation, all of these factors cancel each other out, leaving this: Any time of year is a fine time to visit Trinidad and Tobago.

HOW TO GET THERE

Most published travel guides list only two international carriers as serving Trinidad and Tobago and neglect to mention British West Indian Airlines (BWIA), which sometimes offers by far the most reasonable prices available. At this time BWIA's telephone number in the U.S. is 800-538-2942. Until early 1995, BWIA was the national airline of Trinidad and Tobago; in 1995 it was acquired by a U.S. investment group. In the U.S. BWIA serves Kennedy International Airport in New York (formerly through the British Airways ticket counter and currently through the American Airlines ticket counter) and Miami International Airport in Florida. In Canada BWIA serves Pearson International Airport in Toronto. In Europe, BWIA serves Heathrow International Airport in London, Frankfurt International Airport in Germany (through the Air Canada ticket counter), and Zurich International Airport (through the Icelandic Airlines ticket counter). All flights to Trinidad land at Piarco International Airport in northcentral Trinidad, with linking flights to Crown Point Airport in Tobago. Many flights stop once, some in Barbados, St. Lucia ("Loo'-sha"), or Antigua ("An-tee'-gah"), and others in Aruba. The flight from Miami lasts about 4 hours, from New York 5-6 hours, and from London 7-8 hours. The flights are usually very smooth, with the aircraft cruising at 32-37,000 feet in altitude (I'll let you figure out how many meters that is).

If you decide to travel with a tour group, the tour company will secure your international airfare at the lowest available rate. If you prefer to travel on your own, any travel agent can work out a GIT (Group Inclusive Tour) package for you wherein you reserve not only your airfare but your ground accommodations for a stipulated minimum number of nights. By so doing you'll be able to secure a round-trip ticket for a greatly reduced price. However, check to determine if other carriers are offering special fares. Use caution, however; some carriers may offer a low fare but then drastically limit your choice of accommodations. During Carnival season, airfares jump in response to the increased demand.

ORGANIZED TOURS

The number of persons registering for birding trips conducted by professional nature tour companies is increasing constantly. The primary advantage of joining such a group is the extreme extent to which your preliminary work is reduced, often to the point of your simply packing your luggage and arranging transportation to and from your hometown airport. Another advantage is the opportunity to enjoy the fellowship of kindred spirits. Points to consider include the experience and reputation of the tour company, the expertise of the leaders and local guides, the reputation and convenience of the accommodations at which you'll be staying, the time of year during which you'll be traveling, and the cost of the trip relative to others of a similar nature. Any reputable bird tour company will gladly send you the names of previous tour participants from whom you can determine to your own satisfaction the quality of their tours.

Since the early 1980s I've been conducting birding tours to Trinidad and Tobago under the auspices of my own nature tour company, Peregrine Enterprises Inc. Without going into too much detail, let it suffice for me to say that our tours are widely acclaimed as among the very best. My associates and I constantly explore the islands for new, better, safer, more spectacular, and more rewarding sites. The list of participants from our trips now numbers in the hundreds.

Besides my tours I also can vouch for the integrity of the following companies that also offer birding trips to Trinidad and Tobago:

CALIGO VENTURES INC.

Although not a birding tour company in the strictest sense, Caligo Ventures (named after the caligo, an eye-spot butterfly found in Trinidad) is at this time the sole international agent for the Asa Wright Nature Center. Included in Caligo Ventures packages are three meals per day; all gratuities except to local leaders, drivers, and boatmen; baggage handling and transportation to and from airports; and a bird checklist. Their tours to Trinidad include five field trips with some of Trinidad's most experienced local guides. Their packages also provide ample time for you to enjoy and explore the Center's 200-acre sanctuary.

Caligo Ventures packages that include Tobago offer two additional field trips, usually led by local expert Adolphus James. Accommodations on Tobago are at the Kariwak Village or the Blue Waters Inn. Price differences among tours reflect high and low seasons and inclusion or exclusion of Tobago. Group and individual reservations at the various properties are accommodated as well as complete tour packages.

Caligo Ventures and the Asa Wright Nature Center present a series of professionally instructed summer seminars designed both to educate and entertain. These programs, aimed at amateurs as well as advanced students, are devoted to nature photography in the tropics and to the study of tropical birds and field natural history. A highlight during the birding year is a special Christmas season package that includes participation in the annual Audubon Christmas Bird Count, conducted and compiled at the Center.

In Trinidad, facilities and accommodations also are available in the Arima Valley at the Simla Field Research Station, which is operated by the Center for bonafide scientific research projects. Contact Caligo Ventures directly for details on this program.

Address —   Caligo Ventures Inc.
              156 Bedford Road
              Armonk, New York 10504 USA
              (800) 327-2753 within New York state
              (800) 426-7781 elsewhere

ECO TOURS

Eco Tours is a Trinidad-based tour company catering to naturalists. The owner, Rajinora Mahabir of Arima, Trinidad, offers sightseeing and natural history trips for those already "in country." Among his destinations are the Asa Wright Nature Center, Caroni Swamp, the mountain El Tucuche (for high elevation species), Guanapo Valley and gorge (seasonal), Hollis Reservoir, Matura Beach (seasonal; nesting sea turtles), Nariva Swamp/Manzanilla Beach, the North Coast Road via the Arima Valley, Oropuche Cave (oilbirds), Paria Bay and waterfall, Pitch Lake, the Tamana Caves (in the Central Range; oilbirds), Toco and Galera Point (far northeast), and the Pointe-à-Pierre Wild Fowl Trust. Eco Tours also conducts daily trips into the Caroni Bird Sanctuary.

Conservationists find it very heartening when local companies begin to recognize ecotourism as a profitable avenue to follow. My hope is that other entrepreneurs in Trinidad and Tobago will join in seizing the financial opportunities afforded them by the influx of visiting naturalists. Through their prosperity may come an enhanced commitment to local conservation.

Address —   Eco Tours
               #2 Orange Flat
               Arima, Trinidad, W.I.
               (809) 667-0788

PAN CARIBE TOURS

Ms. Paula Beaird is the Director of Pan Caribe Tours, a whole-saler/tour operator that has been specializing in tours to Trinidad and Tobago for 14 years and which has extensive experience in planning tours of all kinds. Pan Caribe Tours puts together trips for travel on any date, with no specific limits on the length of stay on either island. Their tour costs include air, land, and ground transportation. Pan Caribe Tours can customize itineraries to include field trips or any sightseeing you may wish to enjoy. A potential visitor need only phone, and the package will be made up at the lowest overall cost. If you prefer to work through your favorite travel agent, Pan Caribe will work directly with your agent for the same low rate. Office hours are 8:30 a.m. through 5:30 p.m. Central Standard Time and 9:00 a.m. through noon on most Saturdays.

Address —   Pan Caribe Tours
               P.O. Box 3223
               Austin, Texas 78764 USA
               (800) 525-6896 (USA and Canada) voice
               (512) 267-9209/9215 elsewhere, voice

TROPICAL BIRDING ADVENTURES, INC.

Another nature tour company that organizes birdwatching and natural history expeditions to Trinidad and Tobago is Tropical Birding Adventures, a dynamic partnership between two avid and enthusiastic birders: Winston Nanan of Trinidad and Nancy Standley, the com-pany's North American coordinator and business manager. Tropical Birding Adventures offers group tours limited to 10 participants as well as personal-ized, independent itineraries for birders who prefer not to travel with groups.

Discounts are provided for groups of ten. The all-inclusive group package includes six field trips in Trinidad and three in Tobago, all lodging, three meals per day, field trip transportation, baggage handling, airport transfers, and the exclusive services of experi-enced naturalist Winston Nanan on both islands. Winston Nanan possesses considerable knowledge of the entire Caribbean and is eloquent in his narration and observations of wildlife.

An interesting aspect of the Trinidad portion of a Tropical Birding Adventures' trip is that the lodging is split between the Asa Wright Nature Center and an excellent facility in Port-of-Spain. Tropical Birding Adventures Inc. thus maximizes birding time by eliminating the 45-minute drive to and from the Asa Wright Nature Center for field trips south of the Northern Range, especially those to the west of the Arima Valley.

Address —   Tropical Birding Adventures, Inc.
               P.O. Box 81888
               Chicago, Illinois 60681 USA
               (800) 462-2473 ("GO 2 BIRD") voice

IMMIGRATION AND CUSTOMS

Entering and leaving Trinidad and Tobago is relatively painless. You'll complete an immigration card during the last leg of your incoming flight. **Don't discard this document** after your arrival because you must surrender it upon your departure. After landing, passing through an immigration line, and securing your luggage, you can follow the Green Line through Customs if you have nothing to declare. You're eligible to use the Green Line if you're not importing fresh vegetables, fruit, firearms, narcotics, pornography, or excessive amounts of alcohol. Visitors are allowed to import 50 cigars, 200 cigarettes or one pound of tobacco, and one quart of distilled spirits. Nearly all visitors qualify for the Green Line and pass through without delay. You need not declare binoculars, telescopes, cameras, video cameras, and other optical equipment.

Remember to reserve the equivalent of TT$75 during your stay to pay your airport departure tax. This payment may be made in either TT$ or in US$ at this time.

Every visitor must possess a valid passport. Although no formal agreement exists, citizens of Venezuela or the United States who are seeking entry exclusively for vacation purposes don't require visas for stays of 1) two weeks or less for Venezuelans or 2) two months or less for U.S. citizens. If your stay exceeds six weeks, you must obtain a tax clearance before departing Trinidad and Tobago. A tax clearance may be obtained for TT$30 at the tax office on the corner of Queen and Edward Streets in Port-of-Spain.

Citizens of the United States who lack a valid passport should apply for one well in advance of their trip. First-time applicants must appear in person at a local courthouse or post office. If you've owned a passport, you may be able to renew it by mail through your regional Passport Services agency or through the Washington

Passport Agency, 1111 19th Street NW, Washington, DC 20036. A recorded message is available at the Office of Passport Services in Washington at (202) 647-4814. You also may find U.S. Department of State Publication 9458 to be of use.

Entry visas also aren't required for citizens of Commonwealth countries, with the exception of Australia, India, New Zealand, Nigeria, Papua New Guinea, Sri Lanka, Tanzania, and Uganda. Pakistan is treated as a Commonwealth country for visa purposes.

Citizens of the following countries must obtain visas prior to their entry into Trinidad and Tobago: Albania, Bulgaria, Cuba, all of the former Czechoslovakian states, Hungary, North Korea, the Peoples Republic of China, Poland, the Republic of China (Taiwan), Yugoslavia, Romania, all of the states of the former USSR, and Vietnam.

Residents of the United States may take home purchases totaling US$400 without paying duty. Family members living in the same household may pool their exemptions. You may also mail home items worth up to US$50 duty-free, except spirits, tobacco, or perfume.

WHERE TO STAY

If independent birding is more your style than is a guided tour, you should reserve your own accommodations well in advance of your visit. The usual problem in the tropics is finding a place where you can operate in reasonable comfort and still find wildlife in the immediate area. Although you can find myriads of hotels and guest houses in Trinidad and Tobago, many with fine reputations and choice locations, only those that are most popular with birders are listed below. The Pax Guest House Mount St. Benedict and the Asa Wright Nature Center are both topnotch places to stay. Both places welcome birders and other adventurers traveling without a group. Be sure to call or write for current rates.

IN TRINIDAD —

ASA WRIGHT NATURE CENTER

The Asa Wright Nature Center, the former Springhill Estate, is located in the Northern Range at an elevation of 360m, 12km north of the city of Arima. Formerly a cocoa-coffee-citrus plantation, it's now a wildlife sanctuary, covered mostly by reclaimed secondary forest largely surrounded by impressive tropical rainforest. Several 18 kilometers of trails offer spectacular birding opportunities. The

Veranda of the Asa Wright Nature Center. One of the most popular birding sites in Trinidad because of the bird feeders just below the windows.

food at the Center includes many delicious local specialties, served buffet style. Traditional afternoon tea is served, often enlivened by the anvil-like chorus of bearded bellbirds from the valley below. Before dinner, complimentary rum punch is served on the veranda to guests. A true retreat, no telephone is available at the Center, but public phones are available in Arima, a 15-minute drive down the mountain. The Center maintains constant contact with its Arima office by means of short-wave radio (coming soon: cellular phones).

Electricity at the Center is standard 120-volt, 60-cycle alternating current. Some rooms are in the estate house, and the rest are in separate bungalows. All rooms have private baths with shower. Meal times are standard, and excellent picnic lunches are arranged for field trips.

Address —   The Manager
             Asa Wright Nature Center and Lodge
             P.O. Box 4710
             Arima, Trinidad, W.I.
             (809) 667-4655 voice
             (809) 667-0493 fax

or

Caligo Ventures Inc.
156 Bedford Road
Armonk, NY 10504 USA
(800) 327-2753 (within New York state) voice
(800) 426-7781 (elsewhere) voice
(914) 273-6370 fax

PAX GUEST HOUSE MOUNT ST. BENEDICT

At the edge of the Northern Range, with the ornate tapestry of the blue-green forest on Mount Tabor at its back and the lush Plains of Caroni at its feet, lies the Pax Guest House Mount St. Benedict . Centrally located in the cool heights (250m) of the largest and oldest (1912) Benedictine monastery in the Caribbean, it boasts 19 rooms, three tennis courts, and nature trails on a 600-acre estate. The area contains two distinctly different types of evergreen forest: softwood (Caribbean pine) and hardwood. Guided tours through the estate are available. The Pax Guest House Mount St. Benedict is only five minutes from the campus of the University of the West Indies (UWI; pronounced "you'-ee"). The proximity of the Guest House to UWI, combined with the availability of basic laboratory and conference facilities in the guest house, makes Pax a perfect base for visiting scientists.

Pax Guest House Mount St. Benedict is centrally located for birding excursions in all directions and is itself surrounded by bird-rich habitat. The manager, Mr. Gerard Ramsawak, is the epitome of a perfect host, providing delectable Caribbean dishes, sumptuous lunches, and sublime rum punch while adding his own charming personality to an already pleasing ambiance. You may telephone the Guest House directly from overseas, and you may telephone overseas from the Guest House. Piarco Airport is about 11km to the east, and Port-of-Spain is 12km to the west.

The electricity at the Guest House is standard 120-volt, 60-cycle alternating current; appliances usually will need no converters. Most rooms are on the second floor. Baths are mostly shared, with separate men's and ladies' rooms. There also are efficiency (self-contained) rooms. Breakfast usually is served from 7:30 to 9:00 a.m., lunch buffet at 12:30 p.m., and dinner buffet at 7:30 p.m. Birders can arrange to have breakfast served as early as 5:30 a.m. or to have fruit and beverages set out for them the night before. Enormous lunches are packed every day for picnics in the field.

The Mount St. Benedict monastery complex overlooking the town of Tunapuna, Trinidad, as seen from the fire tower in the forest above the town of Curepe. The Guest House is the secluded building on the left.

Address —

Pax Guest House Mount St. Benedict
Mount St. Benedict
Tunapuna, Trinidad, W.I.
(809) 662-4084 voice and fax
(809) 645-4232 voice and fax

BLANCHISSEUSE BEACH RESORT (LAGUNA MAR NATURE LODGE & COCOS HUT RESTAURANT)

The Blanchisseuse Beach Resort is an oceanfront retreat for naturalists. Located on the north coast of Trinidad, on the outskirts of the village of Blanchisseuse, the property extends from the sandy beaches of Blanchisseuse Bay up into the mountains of the Northern Range. The lush tropical rainforest is interspersed with cultivated crops such as coconut, cocoa, coffee, citrus, and other fruits. Meandering through the valleys and fed by numerous freshwater springs, the Marianne River flows into the ocean at the northeastern end of the property. At its mouth is a beautiful lagoon that's perfect for swimming.

The Laguna Mar Lodge has six guestrooms, all with private baths and wide balconies, and all are cooled by constant ocean breezes. The nearby Cocos Hut Restaurant is open seven days a week and serves local specialties, especially seafood. Much of the food is grown on the estate.

Address —   Blanchisseuse Beach Resort
                 Gottfried and Barbara Zollna
                 c/o Zollna House
                 12 Ramlogan Development
                 La Seiva, Maraval, Trinidad, W.I.
                 (809) 628-3731 voice
                 (809) 628-3737 fax

SURF'S COUNTRY INN

This popular seafood restaurant in the north coast seaside village of Blanchisseuse offers six guest rooms in adjoining buildings. Surf's is located on a wooded hillside overlooking the Caribbean. The Northern Range is your backyard.

Contact Pan Caribe Tours for further information, current prices, and booking.

WINDRUSH BED AND BREAKFAST

This private home is owned by Mrs. Eminel Cooper. Located not far from Surf's Country Inn in the seaside village of Blanchisseuse, it's a very pleasant, cool, and extremely neat house with a beautiful veranda overlooking the Blanchisseuse coastline. Nearby are several sandy beaches, and not far distant are the nature trails of the Northern Range. Other attractions in the area include the Marianne River, Paria Bay and waterfall, forests of *Mora* trees, and several former cocoa and coffee estates.

Mrs. Cooper also manages a small, very simple two-bedroom bungalow in Blanchisseuse, just across the road from Marianne Beach. Each bedroom has one double and one single bed, a bathroom with shower (cold water only), living/dining area, a patio off the living room, and a kitchen equipped with the necessary utensils. The sea breeze makes air conditioning unnecessary.

Address —   Windrush
                 Paradise Hill, Upper Village
                 Blanchisseuse, Tobago, W.I.
                 (809) 664-6114 voice

or contact Pan Caribe Tours for further information, current prices, and booking.

ARNOS VALE HOTEL

A traditional getaway resort for international travelers, the Arnos Vale Hotel is set in a lush 400-acre estate about 15km from Crown Point Airport. The facilities snuggle down a cluster of gentle slopes to the enchantingly private Arnos Vale Bay. Rooms can be reserved in the estate house, in a beachside facility, or in hillside bungalows. A nature trail on the premises allows birders easy access to several different kinds of habitats.

Address —   Arnos Vale Hotel
                   P.O. Box 208
                   Plymouth, Tobago, W.I.
                   (809) 639-2881/2882 voice
                   (809) 639-4629 fax

BLUE WATERS INN

At the northern tip of Tobago and certainly in one of the most secluded parts of the island, the Blue Waters Inn has been a tradi- tional alternative to the more sporty resorts at the southern end of Tobago. This cozy, easy-going, informal divers' and birders' haven is hidden in the cove of Batteaux Bay, facing Little Tobago Island. The Blue Waters Inn has 38 guest rooms, four of which are self- catering. Two of the guest rooms have living room, kitchen, and either one or two bedrooms. The Inn also offers a tennis court and an intimate bar with a television. Birds of several species fly through the dining room, which is ornamented with driftwood, sea fans, and sea shells. Ceiling fans and sea breezes cool the rooms, making air conditioning unnecessary. Complimenting its convenient location near the Main Ridge rainforests and Little Tobago Island, the Blue Waters Inn offers birding in 40 acres of lit- toral woodland and along oceanfront trails.

Address —   Blue Waters Inn
                   Speyside, Tobago, W.I.
                   (809) 660-4077 voice
                   (809) 660-5195 fax

COCRICO INN

The Cocrico Inn is a simple, inexpensive, family-run hotel about 10km from the airport, just south of the Arnos Vale Hotel. It's located in the town of Plymouth, a typical Tobagonian fishing community, where the visitor has an opportunity to converse with "real" Tobagonians. The managers, Nick and Bev Sanford, are from the United States and know what birders like in the way of amenities. All rooms have private bath and shower. Early breakfasts are no problem.

Address —
Cocrico Inn
North & Commissioner Streets
P. O. Box 287
Plymouth, Tobago, W.I.
(809) 639-2961 voice
(809) 639-6565 fax

GRAFTON GREAT HOUSE

Grafton Great House, on Grafton Estate, is located on the leeward (Caribbean) side of Tobago near the village of Black Rock. This 1930s plantation house was home to Eleanor Alefounder. According to the present manager (Mrs. Margretta McWilliam of Cumbria, England), Mrs. Alefounder had a lifelong interest in wildlife and conservation. After Hurricane Flora devastated Tobago in 1963, destroying the birds' habitat and natural food, Mrs. Alefounder did what she could to help feed the birds around her. Starvation brought to her estate house many species that normally would've been too shy to be seen easily. Mrs. Alefounder continued to feed the birds daily on her 200-acre estate, especially in the immediate vicinity of the house. The proximity of so many birds fearlessly coming to her veranda attracted visitors from all over the world. On my first visit I was astonished at the number of species that flew in one side of the house and out the other, as if it were no more than a natural feature of the surrounding woodlands. Bananaquits, blue-crowned motmots, and rufous-vented chachalacas in particular could be hand-fed, with the motmots showing a decided preference for cheese.

Mrs. Alefounder died in 1983 after asking the Trustees to continue her good work, which they've endeavored to do. The copra shed near the house has been restored and converted into an observation center, where you can watch and film birds such as rufous-vented chachalacas and blue-crowned motmots. The former wagon trails through the copra plantation are kept reasonably clear of brush and now are used as nature trails. The major portion of the estate was left to be a bird and wildlife sanctuary for all time, while the house was left to Mrs. Alefounder's family. Grafton Great House is essentially a beloved family home, but between family visits it's rented to ornithologists and to those who appreciate peace and tranquility. The house has been renovated in such a way as to maintain its original appearance.

Rental includes the entire house, which contains three large bedrooms with an additional small bedroom for a child. The living and dining areas are spacious, with nicely polished wooden floors. The kitchen is also large and fully equipped. For a small additional charge, a maid is available to cook and clean. Modern laundry facilities also are available. The trails on the grounds are clearly marked and lead to areas inhabited by such Tobago specialties as blue-backed manakin and olivaceous woodcreeper. Enormous trees near the great house are festooned with night-blooming *Cereus* cactus. The elevated site of the great house takes advantage of cooling sea breezes and affords magnificent views of Stonehaven and Courland Bays and the villages of Black Rock and Plymouth. The garden is secluded, with terraced lawns and an orchard. The beach is about 0.3km away and is easily accessible by foot or car.

Address —   Grafton House
               Black Rock, Tobago, W.I.
               022-971-6568/6721 voice and fax (U.K.)

or contact Pan Caribe Tours for further information, current prices, and booking.

KARIWAK VILLAGE

The Kariwak Village is a delightful, intimate, very American hideaway within walking distance of Crown Point Airport. In addition to serving some of the most savory food in Tobago, the Kariwak offers a swimming pool, live music on Friday and Saturday nights, and early breakfasts for birders. The birding world has discovered this place, and it's now a necessity that you reserve your room months in advance. It's worth the effort. The manager, Cynthia Clovis, constantly finds ways to improve the already excellent ambience. For years she has maintained the Kariwak Village as a dependable home-away-from-home for scores of bird tour companies. Ms. Clovis can provide you with timely advice on what is happening islandwide and can arrange field trips for you with local birding experts such as Adolphus James and David Rooks.

Address —   Kariwak Village
               P.O. Box 27
               Scarborough , Tobago, W.I.
               (809) 639-8442 voice
               (809) 639-8441 fax

PALM TREE VILLAGE

One of the newest facilities in Tobago, the Palm Tree Village resort features both independent villas (two or four bedrooms) and 20 luxury twin hotel rooms, along with a restaurant, swimming pool, bar, conference rooms, tennis court, and horseback riding. The octagonal villas have fully equipped kitchenettes, air-conditioned bedrooms, satellite television and movie channels, spacious living rooms, and ample patio space. The Palm Tree Village is located at the southeastern tip of Tobago on the windward (Atlantic) side. Activities available include dancing, golf, tennis, swimming, snorkeling, scuba diving, waterskiing, and sport fishing. A particularly interesting feature is the 3 kilometers of untouched beach and the coral reef that begins just outside the main building.

Address —   Palm Tree Village
             P.O. Box 327
             Scarborough, Tobago, W.I.
             (809) 639-4347/8/9 voice
             (809) 639-4180/623-5776 fax

RICHMOND GREAT HOUSE

This beautifully restored British sugar-plantation mansion is located in Belle Garden on the windward (Atlantic) side of Tobago, high atop a lofty hill that provides fine views in all directions. This elegant house dates from 1766 and includes five bedrooms, a restaurant, a bar, and a pool. The interior is dark mahogany with high, white ceilings, huge rooms, and early 20th-century furniture. It houses a collection of African sculptures and carvings. The vista is one of flowers, mature fruit trees, rolling coastal hills, and the unbroken forest of the highlands as far as the eye can see.

Address —   Richmond Great House
             Belle Garden, Tobago, W.I.
             (809) 660-4467 voice

or contact Pan Caribe Tours for further information, current prices, and booking.

SEA EDGE BED AND BREAKFAST

This private, spacious, ranch-type home is located in Mount Irvine on the leeward (Caribbean) side of Tobago. The view over Buccoo Reef provides magnificent vistas of brilliant sunsets as well as seasonal sightings of porpoises and marine turtles. The Sea Edge is near Grafton Estate with its abundant birdlife. The Sea Edge is very intimate, offering just two apartments, one a two-bedroom, the other a one-bedroom.

Address —   Sea Edge
c/o Scarborough Post Office
Scarborough, Tobago, W.I.
(809) 639-3926 voice

or contact Pan Caribe Tours for further information, current prices, and booking.

SPEYSIDE INN

This family-run establishment is located on the windward (Atlantic) side of Tobago on the outskirts of the tiny northern village of Speyside. All five comfortable guest rooms, with their terra-cotta floors, face out on the Atlantic Ocean. Each room has its own balcony and private bathroom. The Speyside Inn was rebuilt from a beautiful old white frame house that was owned by the publisher of Trinidad's **Field Naturalist** magazine. Just down the hill is Batteaux Bay across from Little Tobago Island, while behind the inn rise the foothills of Pigeon Peak, Tobago's highest point. The Rainforest Reserve is a mere 20-minute drive away. The owners of the Speyside Inn are conservationists who take pride in their fine cuisine, which they serve on their romantic sea grape terrace.

Address —   The Speyside Inn
Windward Road
Speyside, Tobago, W.I.
(809) 660-4852 voice and fax

or contact Pan Caribe Tours for further information, current prices, and booking.

TURPIN'S (MAN O' WAR BAY) COTTAGES

Charles and Pat Turpin rent six beachside houses near Charlotteville, the northernmost town in Tobago. This is an ideal setting for nature lovers, as the cottages are on the Charlotteville Estate, a 1,000-acre former cocoa plantation. The entire estate is open to visitors who may wander in freely from the beach, among cocoa trees and right into the rainforest. From Turpin's Cottages, a 5-minute walk along the beach takes you to the petite fishing village of Charlotteville, with its local shops, markets, rum shops, and local restaurants. Turpin's lies between two premier birding attractions, St. Giles (Goat) Island Bird Sanctuary and Little Tobago (Bird of Paradise) Island Bird Sanctuary. The managers arrange and guide birding and nature field trips. The cottages are surrounded by colorful landscaped grounds that comprise a tropical garden of beautiful shrubs and flowers.

The simple accommodations, located near the beach, are airy and spacious, with one 1-bedroom cottage, three 2-bedroom cottages, one 3-bedroom cottage, and one 4-bedroom cottage. Each cottage is comfortably furnished with a living room, dining area, kitchen with all utensils, a bathroom with hot and cold water, screened and louvered windows, and fans. The cool sea breeze makes air conditioning unnecessary. In front of each cottage is a veranda with lounging chairs. For a small additional charge, you can secure the services of a maid to cook and clean. A dive shop provides snorkeling and scuba equipment. An honor-system commissary provides domestic supplies for those who choose to cook for themselves. Fresh fish is available when the local fishermen bring their catch to the Charlotteville fish house, and local Charlotteville markets supply vegetables and other foodstuffs. Drivers and boatmen are available for excursions throughout the island of Tobago or to nearby St. Giles and Little Tobago Islands.

Address —   Charles and Pat Turpin's Cottages
                 Charlotteville, Tobago, W.I.
                 (809) 660-4327 voice
                 (809) 660-4328 fax

OTHER FACILITIES

Visiting birders also have reported favorably about the following mostly larger and less nature-oriented properties. For a current list of accommodations, eating places, other information useful to visitors, request a copy of **Discover Trinidad & Tobago** from Trinidad and Tobago Tourism Services.

In Trinidad:

 ALICIA'S HOUSE (St. Ann's, in Port-of-Spain)
  (809) 623-2802 voice (809) 623-8560 fax

 HALYCONIA INN (Cascade, near Port-of-Spain)
  (809) 623-0008 voice (809) 624-6481 fax

 HOLIDAY INN (Port-of-Spain)
  (809) 625-3361 voice (809) 625-4166 fax

 KAPOK HOTEL (Port-of-Spain)
  (809) 622-6441 voice (809) 622-9677 fax

LA BELLE MAISON (Maracas)
(809) 663-4413 voice   (809) 642-1076 fax

NORMANDIE HOTEL (St. Ann's, in Port-of-Spain)
(809) 624-1181 voice and fax

PAR-MAY-LA'S INN (Port-of-Spain)
(809) 628-2008 voice   (809) 628-4707 fax

S&D HOUSE (Arouca)
(809) 642-3659 voice   (809) 642-1076 fax

TROPICAL HOTEL (Maraval, near Port-of-Spain)
(809) 622-5815/4249 voice   (809) 628-3174 fax

VALSAYN VILLA (east of Port-of-Spain)
(809) 645-1193 voice and fax

ZOLLNA HOUSE (Maraval)
(809) 628-3731 voice   (809) 627-0856 fax

In Tobago:

ARTHURS BY THE SEA (near Crown Point)
(809) 639-0196 voice   (809) 639-4122 fax

CHOLSON CHALETS (Mount Pleasant, near Charlotteville)
(809) 639-8553/2847

CONRADO BEACH RESORT (Pigeon Point)
(809) 639-0145/6 voice   (809) 639-0755 fax

GRAFTON BEACH RESORT (Black Rock)
(809) 639-0191 voice   (809) 639-0030 fax

JIMMY'S HOLIDAY RESORT
(809) 639-8292/8929 voice   (809) 639-3100 fax

PLANTATION BEACH VILLAS LTD. (Black Rock)
(809) 639-0455 voice and fax

SEA BREEZE MOTEL (Scarborough)
(809) 639-6404 voice   (809) 639-5158 fax

BED AND BREAKFASTS

The concept of a bed-and-breakfast for birders has been a long time coming to Trinidad and Tobago. But when you stop and think of it, what do birders really want, except for a comfortable bed and decent facilities for cleaning up. Most often we leave the jacuzi, hot tub, dance floor, and bar to more "normal" folks.

For a current list of bed-and-breakfasts, contact the following organizations:

Bed & Breakfast Association of Trinidad and Tobago
P.O. Box 3231
Diego Martin, Trinidad, W.I.
(809) 669-2577/637-9329/663-4413 voice
(809) 627-0856 fax

Tobago Bed and Breakfast Association
c/o Federal Villa
1-3 Crooks River
Scarborough, Tobago, W.I.
(809) 639-3926/8836 voice   (809) 639-3566 fax

TRANSPORTATION IN TRINIDAD AND TOBAGO

Traveling in Trinidad and Tobago is easy. Taxis abound everywhere except in the most remote locales, even late at night. Buses adhere to regular schedules along all highways and offer extremely reasonable fares, often less than TT$1 for long distances.

All license plates in Trinidad and Tobago begin with one of four letters: H (for hire), T (truck), P (personal vehicle), or R (rental).

You may stand on the roadside and flag down any vehicle displaying an H-plate. Taxi fares are somewhat higher than are bus fares, but for-hire vehicles (taxis) are much more common than buses, and the fares are still good deals. H-plate vehicles sometimes travel along specific routes

Typical maxi-taxi.

and therefore may not deliver you precisely to your destination. Drivers will drop you off at major intersections, where you can secure another taxi to take you the rest of the way to your destination. Alternatively you may be able to negotiate with a driver to take you to your destination for an additional fee.

Officially designated minibuses ("maxi-taxis") also are fairly easy to find. As with other H-plate vehicles, maxi-taxis follow regular routes and stop wherever potential passengers flag them down. Fares are somewhat lower for maxi-taxis than are those for taxis.

Here's an actual comparison from 1990 (prices will now be higher but the relative costs should be similar). From the Pax Guest House Mount St. Benedict to Port-of-Spain (about 15km), I first secured transportation for about TT $2 down the hill to the Eastern Main Road. The bus fare from there to Port-of-Spain was a mere TT 50¢. A taxi fare for the same distance was about TT $8, whereas the fare for a maxi-taxi fare was about TT $5.

A short walk often can save you a considerable amount of money. For example, the fixed taxi rate from Piarco Airport to the Pax Guest House Mount St. Benedict currently is TT$40. However, if you carry your bags to the airport feeder road and flag down a roving H-plate vehicle, the fare is TT $6 for the same trip — a big savings. Be forewarned that this practice won't curry favor with the airport taxi drivers, and you didn't hear it from me.

Many people find it enjoyable and worthwhile to leave the driving to a professional and concentrate instead on observing birds along the road. The manager at your accommodations will be happy to recommend a driver and will even secure such services for you if you so desire.

DRIVING IN TRINIDAD AND TOBAGO

Driving in Trinidad and Tobago is performed in the British style, proceeding on the left side of the road. If you rent a car, you absolutely must spend a few minutes practicing driving in a quiet area such as the back of the airport parking lot before venturing onto the roads. In particular, try to acquire a keen feel for the width of your car. You most certainly will be passing vehicles parked on your left as traffic approaches you on the right. After driving without incident for 20 years in the United States, I had two minor accidents involving parked cars on my first day of driving in Trinidad. I considered myself fortunate not to have had more. Please take a few minutes to familiarize yourself with the right-hand steering wheel and note the location of the gearshift and directional signals. The good news for non-British-style drivers is that the arrangement of the clutch, foot brake, and accelerator is identical regardless of the position of the steering wheel. Be sure to watch carefully *on the left,* not on the right, for road signs and stop lights. Especially important, watch what other drivers are doing before you commit to making a turn after you arrive at an intersection of a divided highway.

Note the white mileposts along many of the roads. The bars under the mile numbers represent quarter miles.

Be aware that it's no disgrace to bring your vehicle to a complete stop if you're confused or unsure of your ability to pass a parked car in the face of oncoming traffic. Oncoming traffic respects a cautious driver and will take pains to avoid colliding with you. In fact, you'll see many vehicles stopped in the roadway, even in heavy traffic, while the driver chats with friends on the sidewalk. Passing the time in this manner is called "liming."

A final word of advice — don't pick up hitchhikers under any circumstances unless you personally know the individuals. "Catching a drop" is a popular way of traveling in Trinidad and Tobago, but leave this practice to the residents.

Visitors in possession of valid licenses issued in the U.S., Canada, France, the U.K., Germany, and the Bahamas may drive legally under that license in Trinidad and Tobago for as long as three months. International motor vehicle licenses also are accepted. Rental agency personnel can advise you about current regulations.

RENTING A CAR

If you feel adventurous and independent, renting a car may be just "de t'ing" for you. Be sure to ask for the maximum amount of insurance available. Get a late-model vehicle with air conditioning and an automatic transmission if you can. You'll pay slightly more for a car with these options, but you'll appreciate the automatic transmission on the mountain roads and the air conditioning in city traffic and in the lowlands. Make sure that the car you rent is equipped with an inflated spare tire and a working jack. Take a few minutes to review the completed rental agreement. Verify that all existing damage to the vehicle (scratches, dents, missing hubcaps) is properly noted in writing on the rental agreement before you leave the rental agency. If the gas tank isn't full, top it off at your very first opportunity. **Gas stations are closed for most or all of the day on the following public holidays:** New Year's Day (January 1), Carnival (the Monday and Tuesday before Ash Wednesday), Good Friday (the Friday preceding Easter), Easter Monday (the day after Easter), Whit Monday, Corpus Christi, Labor Day, Emancipation Day (August 1), Independence Day (August 31), Republic Day (September 24), Christmas Day (December 25), Boxing Day (December 26), Eid Ul Fitr (moveable), and Festival Divali (moveable).

To repeat my previous suggestion — practice driving before hitting the highways.

Airports usually are the most logical places to rent a car. You're then free to roam as you please and can return it conveniently just before your homeward flight. Prices vary somewhat from vendor to vendor. At this time a subcompact such as a Nissan March with standard shift and no air conditioning rents for about TT$207 per day from Auto Rentals, with no deposit required. A Nissan Sentra with automatic transmission and air conditioning from the same vendor rents for TT$258 per day. Insurance costs about TT$21 per day. Prices at other agencies are almost identical but some agencies (such as Singh's Auto Rental) require you to leave a TT$1,000 deposit. Nearly all rental companies give you the seventh day free; you pay only for the seventh day of insurance. Renters are required to be 25 years of age or older, possess a valid driving permit, and have a minimum of three-years driving experience.

The following car rental companies are located at Piarco International Airport or near Crown Point International Airport. I've found them to be friendly, fairly priced, and reliable:

In Trinidad (all at Piarco International Airport) —

Auto Rentals (AR)	(809) 669-2277 ("669-CARS")
Singh's Auto Rentals Ltd.	(809) 664-5417
Lord Kalloo Rental & Taxi Service	(809) 669-5673

On Tobago —

Auto Rentals (AR)	Crown Point (809) 639-0644
Peter Gremli's Car Rental & Transport Service	Crown Point (809) 639-8400
Rattan's Car Rental	Crown Point (809) 639-8271
Singh's Auto Rentals Ltd.	Grafton Beach Hotel (809) 639-0191
Toyota Rent-a-Car	Milford Road (809) 639-7491

BIRDING GUIDE SERVICES

In areas foreign to you, especially if you're birding independently, the services of a local birding guide can be invaluable. In a single day afield in Trinidad with a skilled guide, you can learn scores of bird songs and identification clues. This knowledge will be immediately useful in helping you to avoid spending time stalking common species, or missing a vocal but out-of-sight rarity. In addition to knowing the birds, local guides can point out congregation sites or note special behaviors of interesting species. In Trinidad, and

even more so in Tobago, being seen in the company of a local guide can warm the local people toward you in remote areas where outsiders are few.

Over the years I've ventured afield with some of the best native birding guides in Trinidad and Tobago. In the earlier versions of this book I mentioned a scant three native guides. As the number of visiting birders has increased, so has the number of accomplished birding guides.

Jogie Ramlal, Rudal Ramlal, and Winston Nanan for years have served as the native guides of choice on Trinidad. Jogie is an excellent all-around landbirding guide. Having lived for many years in the Arima Valley and having led

Jogie Ramlal, native guide in Trinidad.

field trips numbering in the thousands to all parts of Trinidad, his knowledge of the songs, habits, and haunts of Trinidad's birds is extensive. He has discovered several species new to the island. His peaceful, friendly demeanor, remarkable serenity, and fine sense of humor make him a wonderful companion in the field.

Equally important, Jogie quickly admits any uncertainly in his identifications, a trait that allows visiting birders to share in discoveries of unusual species (and a trait which all too many birding guides lack). Jogie is one of several guides currently utilized by the Asa Wright Nature Center.

Rudal Ramlal also lives in the Arima Valley just down the road from the Asa Wright Nature Center and thus grew up with the birds we visitors seek. He exhibits all of the fine traits of his brother Jogie. As another of the guides utilized by the Asa Wright Nature Center, Rudal has learned a great deal about the birds of Trinidad over the years. With his easy laugh and quick wit, he also has learned how to keep Americans happy on birding trips. Between the two of them, Jogie and Rudal Ramlal probably have shown more species of birds to more visiting birders than have all the other guides combined. In fact, I once suggested to the Trinidad government that "Ramlal Road" supplant the name Blanchisseuse Road in their honor, there not being one person in fifty who can spell the latter name correctly without vexacious practice and endless repetition.

Winston Nanan is the acknowledged expert on the flora, fauna, and especially the avifauna of the Caroni Swamp Bird Sanctuary. He is widely renowned for his comprehensive knowledge of, and eloquence in describing, not only the birds of the Caroni Swamp but also its plants and other non-avian fauna. Winston has spent his life close to his primary birding area and thus has an unmatched and intimate knowledge of the Caroni Swamp. In addition, he is one of the few native naturalists who is equally familiar with the fauna and flora of Tobago, along with that of other Caribbean and Central and South American countries such as Belize, Costa Rica, Venezuela, and Guyana. An avid ornithologist, wildlife photographer, and cinematographer since his early teens, Winston has a great love for his work and a strong desire to share his knowledge with his clients.

The association of Nanan Tours' with the Caroni Swamp spans half a century. Winston Nanan, who currently heads the enterprise, is the acknowledged expert on the avifauna of the Caroni. An outspoken proponent of wetland conservation, he's well versed in the natural history of the entire Caroni Swamp ecosystem — its mangrove and other forms of vegetation, all manner of vertebrate and invertebrate life, and the sad saga of human impact on the swamp ecosystem. In the tradition of his father, and to ensure a smooth transition to his new tour company (Tropical Birding Adventures Inc.), in 1993 Winston brought his sons Lester and Victor under his tutelage to learn the business and the natural history of the Caroni.

Besides the persons mentioned above, all of whom have proven themselves over the years to be reliable and talented guides in Trinidad, a new generation of exceptionally gifted young naturalists is being groomed as nature tour guides. Among the best of them are guides associated with the Asa Wright Nature Center, such as Kenny Calderon, Vishnu Debe, and Sheldon Driggs.

One of my favorite birding companions in Trinidad is Trevor Yip-Hoi. Trevor is an exceptional all-around naturalist, another of these young, next-generation wonders like Kenny, Vishnu, and Sheldon. Trevor serves as a naturalist / birding guide for the Pax Guest House Mount St. Benedict in addition to his biological research, which includes preparing environmental impact statements. On tours based at Pax Guest House Mount St. Benedict , I use Trevor as our local nature expert whenever possible.

During the revision of this guide, it was necessary for me to call upon the expertise of various Trinidadians to flesh out certain sections. Trevor's generous contributions throughout this edition can be recognized in part by the delightful humor he imparts to what otherwise would have been factual but rather lackluster material. Trevor also revised several of the original area maps and prepared some brand new ones for this edition.

Years ago, when I first began visiting Trinidad and Tobago, I had the good fortune to connect with Elias Mitchell. At that time Elias was working at the Asa Wright Nature Center after a long stint as a naturalist near Chaguaramas. Having birded extensively with Elias in Trinidad, it was a twilight-zone experience a few years later when I happened upon him bicycling to the hawkwatch at Cape May, New Jersey, one autumn day. That's how it is with Elias — always finding new frontiers in natural history. Elias now runs his own nature tour / ecotourism company. I've heard very positive reports from his clients about their satisfaction with his arrangements and his personable style.

Roger Neckles is a Trinidadian naturalist best known for his photography. As you browse Piarco Airport in Trinidad or Crown Point Airport in Tobago, you can admire Roger's photographs. Over the last few years I've been pleased to see more and more of his work published in various magazines as well. The photograph of the purple honeycreeper on the next page is an example of the amazingly crisp shots for which Roger is growing famous.

Roger formed his own ecotourism company a few years ago and has been doing a great job. In fact I received e-mail yesterday that read in part, "We had a wonderful time with Roger Neckles." Besides conducting bird tours, Roger is the person to contact if you have a yen to purchase breathtaking photographs of Trinidad birds, flowers, or landscapes. On one of my recent tours, a participant made arrangements early on during the trip to trade, just before leaving Trinidad, his second-edition National Geographic field guide for a print of Roger's stunning head shot of a golden-headed manakin. That print now serves as the focal point in that participant's office.

Purple honeycreeper. Photo by Roger Neckels.

On Tobago, Adolphus James has been the key player in bird tours for more than 20 years. Adolphus faces a challenge that guides in Trinidad don't encounter when trying to attract birds to the observer. On Tobago, imitations of the call of the ferruginous pygmy-owl are completely ignored by the resident species. To overcome this difficulty, Adolphus has made a lifelong study of Tobagonian birds, especially their calls, and can readily imitate and attract virtually all regularly occurring songbirds. His spacious maxi-taxi can accommodate birding groups in real comfort. The windows of the maxi-taxi are curved and continue almost to the roofline, allowing views of the canopy during the sometimes lengthy drives to prime birding spots.

Also on Tobago, David Rooks is available to guide nature tours. David is a former president of the Trinidad and Tobago Field Naturalists Club. He caters to small groups as well as to the very large groups that arrive on cruise ships. David Rooks presents one of the most absorbing and comprehensive wildlife lectures I've ever heard, entitled *"The Natural History of the Island of Tobago."* Don't miss this lecture if you hear that it's being presented while you're visiting Tobago. David Rooks can be reached through the Kariwak Village or any of the larger hotels.

If you happen to be leading a birding group sufficiently adept or adventurous to bird Tobago without the services of an expert bird guide, or if you're unable to secure the services of Adolphus James or one of his sons with a maxi-taxi, I'd highly recommend hiring Peter Moore and his maxi-taxi as your transportation. Adolphus is the person who can take you out birding in his maxi-taxi and coax a skulking Venezuelan flycatcher down from its canopy perch; Peter will simply drive you quickly and safely to the island's top birding spots, where you can locate and identify the birds yourself. Participants on my tours have found Peter to be a delightful companion, a safe driver, and a knowledgeable local. Like Adolphus, Peter maintains his maxi-taxi in like-new condition.

In Trinidad — For landbirding —

Jogie Ramlal
Rudal Ramlal
    Milepost 3-3/4, Blanchisseuse Road
    Arima, Trinidad, W.I.
    (no telephone; contact through Asa Wright Nature Center)

Kenny Calderon
Vishnu Debe
Sheldon Driggs
    c/o Asa Wright Nature Center
    P.O. Box 4710
    Arima, Trinidad, W.I.
    (809) 667-4655 voice
    (809) 667-0493 fax

Elias Mitchell
Trevor Yip-Hoi
    c/o Pax Guest House
    Mount St. Benedict
    Tunapuna, Trinidad, W.I.
    (809) 662-4084 voice and fax
    (809) 645-4232 voice and fax

Roger Neckles
    17 Morne Haven Condominiums
    Gilkes Street
    Morne Coco Road
    Diego Martin, Trinidad, W.I.
    (809) 633-5614

For Caroni Swamp boat tours and other nature tours throughout the southern Caribbean —

Winston Nanan
    Bamboo Grove Settlement No. 1
    Princess Margaret Highway
    Curepe P.O., Trinidad, W.I.
    (809) 645-1305 voice and fax
or
    contact Tropical Birding Adventures Inc.

In Tobago —

Adolphus James
    P.O. Box 346
    Scarborough Post Office, Tobago, W.I.
    or at Crown Point Airport (license HAL 9826)
    (809) 639-2231 voice and fax

Peter Moore
    192 Mora Avenue
    Milford Court
    Bon Accord, Tobago, W.I.
    (809) 639-2312 voice
    (809) 660-2312 answering machine

PHOTOGRAPHY

Most people bring a camera and plenty of film or a video camera with them on their visits to Trinidad and Tobago. Besides capturing memories, recording equipment is indispensable for documenting rarities. Using a video camera is straightforward; just be sure to keep your batteries charged. The use of optical cameras requires much more forethought. For photographing scenery, any lens from 28mm to 200mm is fine. For photographing birds, a minimum focal length of 300mm is needed, and 500mm is even better. Consider bringing a medium-length lens with a 2X or 3X multiplier. For those who like to photograph at dawn or dusk, it might be helpful for you to know that the length of a day at any time of year averages 12 hours, with sunrise and sunset being within about an hour on either side of 6:00 a.m. and 6:00 p.m., respectively. Dawn and dusk are of surprisingly brief duration throughout the tropics.

In general, techniques applicable in temperate zones work in Trinidad and Tobago. A daylight filter must be used to counteract the strong blue component in the sunlight. Even though tropical sunlight is intense, and slow film (ASA 64) is perfectly fine for most outdoor shots, at noon you may find that your $f16$ day becomes an $f1.8$ day when you enter the rainforest. Most photographers therefore carry film ranging in speed from ASA 64 to ASA 400. Film is available in every major town. High quality photographic processing is available in Port-of-Spain and other large cities.

Photographing scarlet ibis flying in to roost at dusk is a serious challenge. For this endeavor you'll need a video camera, or an optical camera with the fastest film you can obtain. When photographing the scarlet ibis, you have three factors with which you must contend — a gently rocking boat, a quickly diminishing light level, and a moving target. Not very many visitors achieve success in this arena, but you may be lucky. Please don't ask your boatman to violate the minimum-approach markings near the roost sites or to race his engine in an effort to agitate the birds. He might do so, to the detriment of the ibis and birders on future visits.

ATTRACTING BIRDS TO THE OBSERVER

Obvious though it may seem, the more you blend in with the environment, the closer the birds will come to you and the more birds you'll see. Dress so as to be inconspicuous, preferably in greens or browns. You're an intruder in an area the birds know well. The less you move or speak, the better will be your chances to observe secretive species.

If you're accustomed to "pishing" to attract birds in the Northern Hemisphere, you may be in for slow birding in Trinidad and Tobago. While some birds may occasionally respond to such a sound, far more will flock to the call of the ferruginous pygmy-owl. To imitate this species, purse your lips and whistle "hoo" about twice a second; the pitch doesn't matter so much as the tempo. You'll hear the real thing soon after reaching Trinidad and then can perfect your mimicry. The imitated whistle, once you learn to produce it correctly, often will bring in the owl itself to peer at you. Tape recordings of other species, made on the spot and played back, are very effective at bringing skulking species into view, but tapes should be played only until the bird appears. In no case should a bird be harassed by lengthy playbacks of its call — you may well drive it from its territory.

From December through March, you may find it interesting to imitate the call of the eastern screech-owl so as to see how many North American migrants you can attract. Wait until the birds around you have tired of your ferruginous pygmy-owl call, then try the screech-owl call. Often two or three species, such as American redstart, northern waterthrush, or prothonotary warbler, will hop out of the bushes and into view after having ignored your earlier efforts.

One little-know fact known to tropical birders is that many tropical species of birds are quite sedentary during the greatest part of the day, using a "sit-and-wait" hunting style. When the preferred insect or other prey appears, they dive quickly, snatch the prey, and return to the same perch or to another perch nearby. If you miss the few seconds of movement, you miss that species of bird.

As an example of the kind of payoff that this kind of patient watching can yield, let me just say that virtually every white-throated spadebill I've ever seen has been bagged through the "sit-and-wait" method, just staying put and watching for a sudden sortie.

The moral of this story is that you must acquire at least this one new birding technique if you are to develop truly awesome tropical birding skills.

TRINIDAD AND TOBAGO
TOURIST BOARD OFFICES

Additional information on Trinidad and Tobago may be obtained from the following offices:

Head Office in Trinidad

> Trinidad and Tobago Tourism Development Authority
> 134-138 Frederick Street
> Port-of-Spain, Trinidad, W.I.
> (809) 623-1932/4; 623-INFO voice
> (809) 623-3848 fax

United States

> Trinidad and Tobago Tourism Services
> c/o Sales, Marketing and Reservations
>   Tourism Services (SMARTS)
> 7000 Boulevard East
> East Guttenberg, New Jersey 07093 USA
> (201) 662-3403   Fax: (201) 869-7628

Trinidad and Tobago Tourism Services
c/o Cheryl Andrews Marketing Inc.
1500 San Remo, Suite 145
Coral Gables, Florida 33146 USA
(305) 663-1660   Fax: (305) 666-9723   (800) 595-1TNT

Canada

Trinidad and Tobago Tourism & Trade Center
York Center
145 King Street West & University Avenue
Toronto, Ontario M5H 1J8, Canada
(416) 367-0390

United Kingdom

(Office closed; for general information contact the
British Embassy, listed below)

EMBASSIES IN TRINIDAD AND TOBAGO OF THE UNITED STATES, CANADA, AND THE UNITED KINGDOM

United States

15 Queens Park West
Port-of-Spain, Trinidad, W.I.
(809) 622-6371.

Canada

Huggins Building
72-74 South Quay
Port-of-Spain, Trinidad, W.I.
(809) 623-4787/7250

United Kingdom

Furness House
90 Independence Square
Port-of-Spain, Trinidad, W.I.
(809) 625-2861

Embassy of Trinidad and Tobago
1708 Massachusetts Avenue, NW
Washington, DC 20036 USA
(202) 467-6490

Red-bellied macaws over royal palms, Nariva Swamp, Trinidad, by Don R. Eckelberry.

TRINIDAD AND TOBAGO EMBASSIES AND HIGH COMMISSIONS IN THE UNITED STATES, CANADA, AND THE UNITED KINGDOM

United States

> Permanent Trinidad and Tobago Mission
>   to the United Nations
> 801 Second Avenue
> New York, New York 10017 USA
> (212) 697-7620

Canada

Consulate for Trinidad and Tobago
P.O. Box 1526, Station B
Ottawa, Ontario, Canada K1P 5R5
(613) 232-2418

High Commission for Trinidad and Tobago
365 Bloor Street East, Suite 1700
Toronto, Ontario M4W 3L4, Canada
(416) 922-3175

United Kingdom

High Commission for Trinidad and Tobago
42 Belgrave Square
London SW 13NT, England
011-44-245-9351

BIRDING IN TRINIDAD

Provided here are detailed descriptions of birding trips you can
make to different parts of Trinidad. By visiting many different
habitats, you'll enjoy a wider variety of wildlife and see more of
the island. For a visit of about one week in duration, I'd recommended that you follow an itinerary such as the following:

Day 1   Grounds of your hotel or guest house and environs —
        learn most of the local birds
Day 2   Blanchisseuse Road from Arima at least to Brasso
        Seco Trace
Day 3   Asa Wright Nature Center/oilbird cave, Lalaja Trace
Day 4   Wallerfield, Aripo Savannah
Day 5   Arena Forest and Nariva Swamp
Day 6   Trincity ponds, Caroni rice fields, and Caroni Swamp

In the following site descriptions, the numbers that follow the
names of the locations are the approximate distances you'll drive
during the course of that foray and the total amount of travel and
birding time you should anticipate spending on that foray.

Most birders visiting Trinidad shun accommodations in bustling
Port-of-Spain, choosing instead to stay at one of the guest houses
east of the capital city. Therefore, in the directions that follow for
Trinidad sites, I'm assuming that you'll begin from some point east
of Port-of-Spain, such as Tunapuna or Arima.

If you're staying in Port-of-Spain, for most trips described here
44 you'll follow the Churchill-Roosevelt Highway east to the starting

point for the selected trip, then follow the directions from there. For trips close to Port-of-Spain, such as to the Port-of-Spain sewage lagoons, you'll be able to obtain directions to the starting point or even to the destination itself from the hotel manager or staff.

UBIQUITOUS SPECIES

The following species of birds are so common, so widespread, and so conspicuous that I will make little further mention of them: cattle egret, black and turkey vultures, ruddy ground-dove, orange-winged parrot, smooth-billed ani, short-tailed swift, yellow-bellied elaenia, tropical pewee, great kiskadee, boat-billed flycatcher, tropical kingbird, bare-eyed thrush, tropical mockingbird, bananaquit, blue-gray and palm tanagers, carib grackle, blue-black grassquit, and yellow oriole.

Throughout this section I use the phrase "the usual species" to refer to those species that respond readily to the call of the ferruginous pygmy-owl: rufous-breasted and tropical house-wren; bare-eyed thrush; rufous-browed peppershrike; chivi vireo; golden-fronted greenlet; blue dacnis; green, purple, and red-legged honeycreepers; bananaquit; white-shouldered, white-lined, silver-beaked, blue-gray, palm, bay-headed, and turquoise tanagers; and violaceous euphonia.

NORTHERN RANGE

ASA WRIGHT NATURE CENTER
30km, 1 day

The Asa Wright Nature Center is located on a ridgeside in the Arima Valley at an elevation of 360m. A former coffee-cocoa-citrus plantation, the Asa Wright Nature Center (formerly called Springhill Estate) has been allowed to return to a wild state and is a grand place to spend a day or a month. Specialties of the Asa Wright Nature Center include bearded bellbird, tufted coquette, a nesting colony of crested oropendolas, a lek of white-bearded manakins, spectacled owl, white hawk, blue-headed parrot, about seven species of hummingbirds, all three species of trogons, golden-olive and chestnut woodpeckers, black-tailed tityra, and most of the tangers and their allies.

To reach the Asa Wright Nature Center, follow the Eastern Main Road to the town of Arima. As you enter Arima from the west, you'll cross a concrete bridge and then pass a sports arena on the right. The first traffic light has a gas station on the left, a bus depot

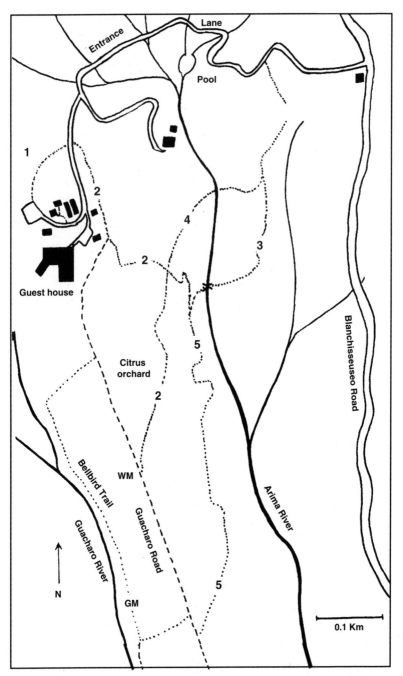

Grounds of the Asa Wright Nature Center. Numbers refer to marked trails. The oilbird colony is in cave along Guacharo River. WM = lek of white-bearded manakin. GM = golden-headed manakin.

on the right, and road signs in front of you that read "No Entry Ahead." At the second traffic light bear left, passing another gas station on the right. After three blocks turn right, at a stop sign, onto Broadway (no street sign). In two blocks you'll arrive at the town center, a "dial" or clock on a pole in the middle of the street. Pass to the left of the dial and take the first left, St. Joseph Street (no street sign). Follow St. Joseph Street through Arima for 1.4km to its junction with the Arima Bypass (North Demerara Road), which merges from the right. The city of Arima ends abruptly here; you're now in a magnificent rainforest, following Blanchisseuse (="washerwoman") Road.

An alternative route, one you might wish to use during periods of heavy traffic, is to follow the Churchill-Roosevelt Highway east instead of the Eastern Main Road, making a left turn at the Arima exit at Demerara Road. Stay on Demerara Road north to the Eastern Main Road, then turn right to the well-marked Blanchisseusse Road. Turn left, thus avoiding most of the congestion in downtown Arima.

Whichever route you chose, you will immediately recognize the change in the envirnment around you when you leave the city of Arima. Continue for about 11km and turn left at the well-marked entrance road to the Asa Wright Nature Center. Follow the rustic "pitch"-paved road to the Center and heed the signs to the visitors' parking lot. The estate house is down the hill .

At the front desk, pay a day-use fee of US$5 and sign the guest book. The Center offers a wide selection of field guides, trail guides, and other books; colorful shirts, decals, and artwork; and other local crafts. Guided walks to Dunstan (Oilbird) Cave are conducted on a scheduled basis; all such business and scheduling is conducted at the front desk. Be sure to pick up a trail map. You may wish to acquaint yourself with other visiting birders and inquire about unusual sightings before beginning your explorations of the Center.

From the veranda of the estate house you can survey the entire length of the Arima Valley and study flying channel-billed toucans, white hawks, and ornate hawk-eagles and obtain very close views or photographs of hummingbirds, tanagers, and honeycreepers at the fruit-filled feeders. Nature trails radiate from the estate house toward several different habitats — along and into the lush rainforest, along the bird-rich entrance road, and to Dunstan Cave, home of the famous oilbird. One very easy and rewarding stroll is along the 1.5-km (round-trip) entrance road. Here you can see bare-eyed, cocoa, and white-necked thrushes; crested oropen-

Switchback on Blanchisseuse Road, one of 387. Excellent area for high elevation and rainforest species.

dola; blue-headed and orange-winged parrots; great antshrike; and squirrel cuckoo.

One of the most popular trails leads downhill from the veranda and passes through a citrus grove where you can see trogons and thrushes. Toucans feed in a towering nutmeg tree, and bearded bellbirds call "BOK!" from the rainforest on the right. At the far side of a grassy clearing, just past at a gigantic mango tree, a clearly defined path leads off to the right. This fairly steep but fascinating trail leads about 2km through a rainforest frequented by such weirdly named birds as gray-throated leaftosser and streaked xenops. The trail ends at the Guacharo River, at the mouth of Dunstan Cave, where the vista encompasses sheer tropical splendor, well worth the hike. From the mouth of the cave birders can usually see a few oilbirds, but in the interest of their continuing habitation you're strongly urged not to disturb them by entering the cave on your own.

While in the ravine, watch for scintillating blue morpho butterflies above and inspect the rock walls of the grotto for nesting chestnut-collared swifts.

Another productive trail at the Asa Wright Nature Center leads past the bungalows above the estate house and connects with the entrance road (0.5km). The forest on the left is home to black-faced

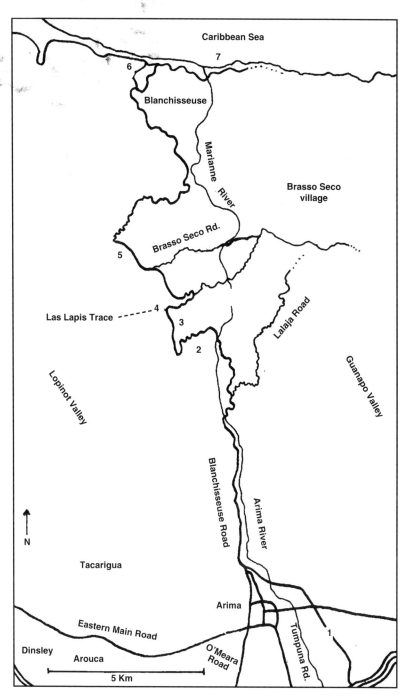

Section of the Northern Range of Trinidad. 1=Arima Bypass, 2=Asa Wright Nature Center, 3=Textel station, 4=high elevation area, 5=overlook for raptors and swifts, 6=Old Blanchisseuse Road, 7=mouth of Marianne River. 49

View of Arima Valley, Trinidad, from Lalaja South Road (=Lalaja Trace). Overlook particularly good for white hawk and bat falcon.

antthrushes, whose imitated whistle often will bring these cryptic, rail-like birds into sight.

BLANCHISSEUSE ROAD
52km, 1 day

A *must* for any naturalist visiting Trinidad is an all-day trip from the town of Arima north along Blanchisseuse Road to the village of Blanchisseuse on the Caribbean coast, or at least as far as Brasso Seco Trace. The following route will take you through some of the most picturesque mountains and highest rainforest on the island. The road itself is thrilling; between Arima and Blanchisseuse are 387 bends and switchbacks; I personally counted them. The vertical roadsides, from which errant vehicles are restrained by wrist-thick bamboo guard rails, are breathtaking with waterfalls and lush vegetation that includes elephant ear and philodendron as well as ferns and mosses.

Between December and March, the mountain immortelle trees are in fiery bloom, coloring the rainforest canopy bright orange and attracting a great variety of nectar-feeding birds and butterflies. You can often observe all three species of trogons along this route as well as white hawk, gray hawk, channel-billed toucan, and golden-headed and white-bearded manakins. The latter two species often display on their communal courts ("leks"). Also possible to see in the heights are speckled tanager, swallow-tanager, bearded bellbird, golden-crowned warbler, and black-faced antthrush. Other species that often are easier to see in the Blanchisseuse Road area than anywhere else in Trinidad include ornate hawk-eagle, green kingfisher, and gray kingbird.

To reach Blanchisseuse Road, follow the directions to the Asa Wright Nature Center as far as to downtown Arima. From the intersection of St. Joseph Road and the Arima Bypass, continue straight ahead into the mountains. The Arima River on the right (0.5km) is a good place to look for kingfishers and gray-headed kites. Pass the Hindu settlement of Temple Village (4.3km) and pull off on the left 0.3km farther. A British-colonial-style concrete bridge marks the beginning of an area especially productive for rainforest birds such as little tinamou, lilac-tailed parrotlet, blue-headed parrot, all of the hermit hummingbirds and the copper-rumped hummingbird, all three species of trogons, blue-crowned motmot, yellow-breasted flycatcher, black-tailed tityra, both species of manakins, rufous-breasted wren, long-billed gnatwren, and crested oropendola. Walk a short distance off the road into the forest on the left and try the call of the ferruginous pygmy-owl to attract the usual species. You can bird the grassy lane on the right side of the road on foot for about 0.5km.

Drive on and turn right at a sign that says "Ramharry Garibdass Bros. Contracting Ltd." (0.3km). This rough track serves as the entrance road to the Simla Research Station. Founded by the

Nest colony of crested oropendola along Lalaja Trace in northern Trinidad.

51

famous naturalist William Beebe, Simla is now managed by the Board of Directors of the Asa Wright Nature Center. Turn left at the gated barrier at the sand quarry (0.4km), park your car, and bird the rest of the entrance road on foot.

Upon returning to your car, drive to the Simla carport (0.6km) and walk up the stairs on the left to the main building. Shout your greetings to make your presence known to the other guests. I've noticed that Trinidad euphonia frequently can be found more easily at Simla than elsewhere. Double-toothed kites have nested in the trees above the carport. Bird the entire Simla area and the trails that lead from the main buildings into the rainforest.

When you have finished birding Simla, return to Blanchisseuse Road and turn right. Stop at as many of the numerous pull-offs as you wish. Turn right when you reach Lalaja South Road (3.0km). The road is steep in places. The views of the Arima Valley alone are worth making this side trip. The many overlooks are great for spotting raptors such as swallow-tailed kite and bat falcon. Walk Cooker Trace, which leads off on the right for 0.3km to its end at a house (0.6km), searching in particular for striped and squirrel cuckoos. Swifts often cross the ridgetop here at knee level, moving from the Arima Valley to the Guanapo Valley and back. Most of them are gray-rumped or band-rumped, but there may be other species mixed in. Your ability to follow a fast-moving swift at close range must be carefully honed before you can make identifications with any certainty.

Ahead 0.2km is a spectacular view of the sparsely inhabited Guanapo Valley to the east; this overlook is particularly good for spotting raptors, with common black-hawk (often in pairs), gray-headed and swallow-tailed kites, bat falcon, and white hawk among the more common species. White-tipped doves and scaled pigeons often streak across the valley, and channel-billed toucans are unmistakable with their woodpeckerlike glides. (Lalaja Bridge Trace ahead 0.5km is too steep for all but vehicles equipped with four-wheel drive, but it provides an invigorating walk to a clearing in the forest.) After crossing a rustic bridge (1.3km), you'll come to Vincent Trace leading off on the right (0.4km), another good birding area. Ahead (0.3km), Lalaja-Paria Trace leads off to the left. Farther on, Lalaja Road deteriorates into an unpaved, rutted path that winds through semi-abandoned coffee-cocoa estates that abound in nesting colonies of crested oropendola. Turn around at Lalaja-Paria Trace and return to Blanchisseuse Road, stopping again at the overlooks if time allows.

Proceed for 2.3km farther up Blanchisseuse Road and scan the rainforest halfway up the far side of the valley for the Asa Wright Nature Center. You can reach the Asa Wright Nature Center property by way of an entrance road on the left (0.3km). Stop and visit or return later for an entire day's birding on the Asa Wright Nature Center grounds.

Pendulous nests of crested oropendolas overhang the road 1.1km ahead. Stop at the powerline clearcut 1.7km farther and enjoy a splendid view of the Arima Valley and the Arena Reservoir and Reservoir far out in the distance and to the right. This overlook is a good spot for observing channel-billed toucan, white hawk, and both species of parrots. Park at the entrance to the Textel microwave station on the right (0.4km). Search the low brush along the entranceway for speckled tanager, which is frequently seen at this spot. Back on Blanchisseuse Road, about 0.5km farther is a good vantage point on the left for viewing the Northern Range Forest Reserve "A" and the Lopinot Valley to the west. I've often found slaty-capped flycatcher here. The tallest peak visible is El Tucuche (="hummingbird"), Trinidad's second-highest point.

Las Lapis Trace/Andrews Trace, on the left across the road from a fenced-in transmitting station, leads into bird-rich rainforest (0.9km). The elevation at this point is 595m, the highest elevation on Blanchisseuse Road. Andrews Trace runs essentially east-west for kilometers in either direction, maintaining an elevation of 455-760m. Plan to spend an hour here looking for the high elevation specialties — orange-billed nightingale-thrush, yellow-legged thrush, and blue-capped tanager — as well as looking and listening for tropical parula and golden-crowned warblers, both of which are common. Birders have seen or heard spectacled owl here in recent years. From October to March, look for migrant North American warblers such as American redstart and northern waterthrush. Note that Las Lapis Trace is closed to vehicles.

At a switchback ahead (1.4km) is a sign that says "Paria-Morne Blue Road, Brasso Seco 4km, Blanchisseuse 12km." You can often hear red howler monkeys along the Paria-Morne Blue Road, so explore the first few kilometers if you wish. However, you probably will already have seen most bird species found there, so continue on Blanchisseuse Road as it switches back to the left. The route is all downhill for the next few kilometers, and the habitat becomes drier and more typically Caribbean. Continue 1.6km to an open, grassy area good at times for yellow-bellied seedeater and sooty grassquit, and recently for a lone indigo bunting. Not far ahead (1.1km), just beyond the spot where Morne La Croix Trace leads off to the left, you'll be treated to a distant view of the hamlet of Morne La Croix itself far below. El Brasso Trace leads off on the

Blanchisseuse Beach on Trinidad's northern coast. Good for sandpipers, plovers, brown pelican, and magnificent frigatebird.

right (0.6km); this is a good trail to walk for ant-associating birds such as plain-brown and buff-throated woodcreepers, great antshrike, plain antvireo, and black-faced antthrush. The spot where Mount La Croix Trace rejoins Blanchisseuse Road on the left can be good for band-rumped swift (1.2km). Within sight on the left ahead (0.1km), in the vanishingly small hamlet of Morne La Croix, is the famous hedge of blue vervain that's mentioned in all travel brochures as frequented by tufted coquette (which I've yet to see there). Ahead 2.5km on the left is another wonderful overlook to the west, good for white, common black-, and zone-tailed hawks and for viewing swifts from above. Collared trogon is often seen 4.1km farther ahead in a delightfully cool valley, shady and birdy, at a bend in the Marianne River.

Old Blanchisseuse Road leads off on the left in 5.0km. Stay to the right and you'll soon be able to congratulate yourself on having successfully negotiated the Andes Mountains (5.4km). You'll see the Caribbean directly ahead as you reach the North Coast Road (1.6km). Turn right, then bear left at 0.9km at the Y intersection. A bathing beach on the left offers a panoramic view of the Caribbean, where brown pelicans and magnificent frigatebirds are abundant (0.7km). Farther down the road, at the end of the pavement, a cable bridge crosses the mouth of the Marianne River, where a sandy, sheltered lagoon provides habitat for spotted and solitary sand-

, ᵣ ₋ːs and as well as American pygmy- and green kingfishers (0.4km). Among the species of birds flycatching over the bridge are gray-breasted martin, southern rough-winged swallow, and short-tailed swift. A trail on the right just before the bridge leads into low-lying woodlands, good for tropical screech-owl and ferruginous pygmy-owl. King vulture, both adult and immature, have been seen in this densely populated area in recent years, perhaps an indication of breeding.

Retrace your route 2.0km to the intersection of Blanchisseuse and North Coast Roads. Just ahead, Lionel Oliver's store on the left offers drinks and especially good currant rolls (0.1km). Scan the power lines in the village for gray kingbird. A right turn 2.2km farther, onto an inconspicuous dirt lane just after a small bridge, provides access to a tiny photogenic beach nestled between rocky headlands. The petite Damier River at the east (right) end of the beach is a reliable site for finding American pygmy-kingfisher.

On your return drive to Arima, you might wish to try Old Blanchisseuse Road (about 0.5km from the beach lane on the right, just before the Police Station), not so much for birding but for the exhilaratingly steep climb and superb views of the Caribbean from the top. Try to spot the island of Tobago far off and on the right, about 50km across the Caribbean. Then retrace your route back to Arima.

HEIGHTS OF ARIPO
32km, 1 day

This trip is recommended for the early morning, when the maximum number of species are active.

The mountain called El Cerro del Aripo is the highest peak in Trinidad, reaching an elevation of just over 915m. Species of birds found only at such high elevations (above 600m) in Trinidad include orange-billed nightingale-thrush and blue-capped tanager. Other species of special interest to be found here include white and zone-tailed hawks; bat falcon; the rare common (Trinidad) piping-guan; chestnut-collared, gray-rumped, and band-rumped swifts; all three hermit hummingbirds and the rare brown violet-ear; collared and white-tailed trogons; chestnut and lineated woodpeckers; gray-throated leaftosser; plain antvireo; black-faced antthrush; bright-rumped attila; black-tailed tityra; short-tailed pygmy-tyrant; bearded bellbird; yellow-legged, cocoa, and white-necked thrushes; swallow-tanager; and red-crowned ant-tanager.

Intersection of Aripo and L'Orange Roads in the Heights of Aripo, Trinidad. Good for bearded bellbird and other high elevation species.

To reach the Heights of Aripo area, drive east from Arima on the Eastern Main Road, passing the Agricultural Research Station on the left. Proceed for 1.8km to Heights of Aripo Road. A sign on the left across the intersection says "To ARIPO VILLAGE 11.2km." Turn left and begin birding immediately, pulling off the narrow road wherever possible, looking and listening for the usual rainforest species as well as little tinamou and black-faced antthrush.

Follow Heights of Aripo Road uphill, ignoring all lesser roads that lead away from this paved but very winding road. At 6.5km you'll reach a bridge on the right that crosses the Aripo River. Continue straight ahead onto L'Orange Road and enter a former coffee/cocoa/citrus plantation. Growing along the road are breadfruit and breadnut trees. Turn right onRuiz Trace (0.4km), a startlingly steep but paved road that leads up to a prime bearded bellbird display area. Drive as far as you dare, but in any case park before the pavement ends; the road is so steep that brakes won't hold your car on the grass near the summit. Bird on foot as far up the mountain as you wish, searching especially for common piping-guan, channel-billed toucan, blue-headed and orange-winged parrots, bright-rumped attila, black-tailed tityra, and bat falcon. In the proper season, all of the species mentioned at the beginning of this section also can be found here.

56 Backing up very slowly and carefully, return to L'Orange Road, turn left, and continue for 0.7km. Park just before crossing a small

High elevation rainforest along Ruiz Trace, Heights of Aripo, Trinidad.

green-and-white concrete bridge of dubious integrity. Walk and bird the stretch of road ahead for about 1.6km, looking for American pygmy- and green kingfishers, channel-billed toucan, all three species of trogons, and all of the thrushes, tanagers, euphonias, and other usual rainforest species. The estate house on the left just past the bridge attracts at least eleven species of hummingbirds: white-chested emerald; little, green, and rufous-breasted hermits; ruby-topaz hummingbird; white-necked jacobin; black-throated mango; blue-chinned sapphire; copper-rumped hummingbird; long-billed starthroat; and the rare brown violet-ear. The larger trees on the right sometimes yield ferruginous pygmy-owl and tropical screech-owl.

Retrace your route to the intersection of L'Orange and Heights of Aripo Roads at the bridge over the Aripo River. Turn left and cross the bridge onto Heights of Aripo Road. Check the watercress ponds on the right for kingfishers (American pygmy- and green) and for the occasional migrant shorebird. Pass through the village of Aripo and at 4.1kmpark at the obvious trailhead on the left (Dandrade Trace). Ignore the private road on the right, which continues only a little father uphill than you can see. Dandrade Trace leads 15km uphill and down through magnificent rainforest. You can actually drive quite far on Dandrade Trace during dry weather. Because the birding here can be so productive, plan to spend as much time walking as possible. Many of the ant-lovingbird species can be found here as well as less specialized migrant species.

If you feel adventurous, hike all the way to the Caves of Aripo to see oilbirds. For this hike I suggest that you hire any one of a number of local guides in Aripo — signs along Heights of Aripo Road will direct you to several. Alternatively, use the site guide in one of the *Nature Trails of Trinidad* books (obtainable at the Asa Wright Nature Center), noting that trails become obscured quickly in the tropics and may be obliterated by fallen branches and other debris.

HOLLIS RESERVOIR
32km, 1 day

As with the Heights of Aripo foray, this trip is recommended for the early morning, when the maximum number of species are active.

Hollis Reservoir is the largest body of water in the Northern Range. It lies about 4km north of the town of Valencia. Its entire catchment is undisturbed, so the pristine rainforest surrounding it hosts many species of birds, including of course those associated with water. This all adds up to a large potential bird list, including many uncommon species. Birds to look for include little tinamou; least grebe; anhinga; white hawk; broad-winged hawk; ornate hawk-eagle (nests on the eastern side); scaled pigeon; green-rumped and lilac-tailed parrotlets; blue-headed and orange-winged parrots; squirrel cuckoo; rufous-breasted and little hermits; black-throated mango; blue-crowned motmot; white-tailed, violaceous, and collared trogons; belted and green kingfishers; channel-billed toucan; lineated and chestnut woodpeckers; white-bellied antbird; white-flanked antwren; gray-throated leaftosser; black-tailed tityra; bearded bellbird; golden-headed and white-bearded manakins; white-winged swallow; white-necked thrush; rufous-browed peppershrike; blue dacnis; red-crowned ant-tanager; and yellow-rumped cacique.

Each person entering Hollis Reservoir is required to possess a permit, which you must obtain in advance from the Water and Sewerage Authority (WASA), Farm Road, St. Joseph, Trinidad, for TT$5.50 each.

To reach the reservoir, travel east from Arima along the Eastern Main Road to the town of Valencia. Stay to the left, leaving the Eastern Main Road (which continues to the right) and following Valencia Road. Travel 0.55km, ignoring two smaller roads on the left. You'll see a small church on the right. About 100m beyond this, on the left, is the road that leads to Hollis Reservoir.

Travel north along this road, ignoring all side roads. After 1.1km you'll arrive at a checkpoint and a pump house on the right. Stop and present your pass to the guards (remember to retain your half of the pass). If no one is around, don't worry — there is a second checkpoint nearer to the dam.

Proceed for 4.0km along a winding road that runs alongside the Quare River. (Although the forest looks tempting to birders, it's best to wait to bird that area until you get to the dam itself or to bird this stretch of the road on your way out. Your goal is to reach the best birding area at the most productive time of day.) You then will pass through a gate and immediately arrive at a series of small buildings on the left. Stop at the last small building and check once more with the personnel there, presenting your pass.

If you proceed another 0.8km you'll arrive at the southern end of the Hollis Reservoir. Park in front of the metal railing just before a small storage shed (with restrooms) and the staff house. Scan the area for least grebe, anhinga, white hawk, ornate hawk-eagle, scaled pigeon, belted kingfisher, channel-billed toucan, parrots and parrotlets, trogons, white-winged swallow, bearded bellbird, and yellow-rumped cacique.

You're now ready to head toward the forest. Proceed along the narrow footpath, keeping the reservoir on the right, past the storage shed. Immediately start birding the forest edges next to the path and also scan across the reservoir (this is very effective because the path is elevated to the equivalent of treetop level on the far side). Watch for Trinidad and violaceous euphonias, turquoise tanagers, little hermit, blue-chinned sapphire, golden-headed manakin, and rufous-breasted wren.

After about 200m the path becomes a grassy trail that leads into the forest. You'll see a large concrete spillway and sluice on the right. Proceed into the forest, birding as you go. After another 200m or so, the trail descends to the tributary; here you cross along the top of a small dam wall (wet feet!) and then ascend into the forest once more. Watch for red-crowned ant-tanager, white-bellied antbird, little tinamou, gray-throated leaftosser, black-faced antthrush, white-bearded and golden-headed manakins, and trogons. Proceed as far as you wish (the trail is about 3km long). Ahead are several treefalls over which you'll need to clamber. The pathway narrows farther on.

When you're through, retrace your route back to your car. To leave the reservoir area, simply retrace your route 5.1km back to Valencia Road, stopping if you wish to bird the forest alongside the Quare River. Turn right at Valencia Road, and in 0.65km you're back at the Eastern Main Road.

FOOTHILLS AND SAVANNAHS

AGRICULTURAL RESEARCH STATION
20km, half day

The Agricultural Research Station is an active cattle ranch and dairy farm a few kilometers east of Arima in the foothills of the Northern Range. The areas of primary birding interest are the extensive wet pastures, brushy hedgerows, and a few huge, isolated trees that serve as strategic vantage points for raptors, especially savanna hawks, peregrine falcons, and merlins.

To reach the Agricultural Research Station, from the Arima area follow the Churchill-Roosevelt Highway east of Tumpuna Road (intersection with traffic lights) and continue for 2km, ignoring a left turn onto Pinto Road after the first kilometer. At this point be on the lookout for two white stone pillars that mark the beginning of a dual carriageway. These pillars also marked the boundary of an American airbase, Fort Reid, during WWII. Continue along this highway, ignoring a left turnoff after 400m (Demerara Road) and another after 2.1km (Mexico Road), but at this point switch on your left turn signal and take the next left turnoff, about 100m farther. The entrance to this road also is marked by two smaller stone pillars. Follow this road for 1.2km, ignoring any side roads. This brings you to an intersection with the Eastern Main Road. Immediately across the road from you is the entrance to the Agricultural Research Station. Carefully cross the major road, proceed into this driveway, and park. Look for savanna hawk and green-rumped parrotlets in the trees that border the road. Flying overhead or feeding in the fields will be shiny and giant cowbirds, carib grackle, yellow-hooded and red-breasted blackbirds, blue-black grassquit, white-headed marsh-tyrant, and pied water-tyrant.

Drive for another 200m, where you'll arrive at a gate/checkpoint. Explain to the guard that you're birdwatching. Drive past the gate and park across from a series of buildings on your left. Get out of your car and survey the fields and the small watering hole just inside the wire fence. Watch for wattled jacana, southern lapwing, and, in the proper season, for least, spotted, pectoral, and solitary sandpipers; collared and semipalmated plovers; ruddy turnstone; and short-billed dowitcher.

From this point on, the most productive procedure is to drive for short distances, stopping and getting out to scan the fields, trees, and open sky along the way. As shown on the map, you may in

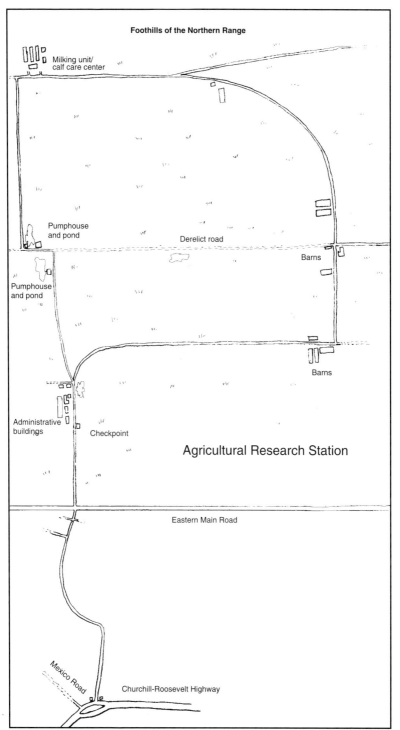

Foothills of the Northern Range

Milking unit/
calf care center

Pumphouse
and pond

Derelict road

Barns

Pumphouse
and pond

Barns

Administrative
buildings

Checkpoint

Agricultural Research Station

Eastern Main Road

Mexico Road

Churchill-Roosevelt Highway

fact complete a circuit drive of the Agricultural Research Station. The clockwise route is described here.

Proceed for about 50m, where the road bends to the right. There are two side roads to the left at this point; ignore the first and turn onto the second. Continue for about 500m, birding as you go. Peregrine falcon, merlin, zone-tailed hawk, common black-hawk, savanna hawk, and yellow-headed caracara hunt over the upper fields. Look closely for the yellow-banded napes on the turkey vultures roosting on the ground in the upper fields; this is characteristic of the Venezuelan race of the turkey vulture. You should now be close to a small pump house and pond on your left. Watch for purple gallinule, common moorhen, and yellow-chinned spinetail, as well as the peering eyes of any caiman that may be cruising about. Just in front of you is a T intersection. The more derelict trail to the right is a useful one to explore on foot as you scan the fields, shrubs, and fence lines for pinnated bittern, great blue and cocoi herons, ruddy-breasted seedeater, southern rough-winged and barn swallows, gray-breasted martin, and stripe-breasted spinetail. Watch out for cow pies!

Proceed back to your car and continue by turning left. In another 150m take a right turn so that you're alongside another pond / pump house — a good spot for pied water-tyrant and white-headed marsh-tyrant if you haven't seen these species before. Continue for 0.8km along this road. (You may see barbed-wire partitions across the road. Don't worry. You may unhitch these and pass through. Just make sure to replace them and mind that you don't get snagged). This will bring you to another T intersection. Turn right, and after about 100m you'll see a series of buildings (a milking station/calf care center) on your left. Stop and cautiously approach this area on foot, paying particular attention to any ground doves. This is a reliable area for the not-so-common common ground-dove.

When you're finished birding around the barns, return to your car and proceed. This stretch is usually good for giant cowbird, which is often seen walking in the pastures on your left. After about 0.7km the road forks. The left branch is a 1-km-long cul-de-sac, with lots of roadside shrubbery; if you have time, check out this area for the elusive bran-colored flycatcher and striped cuckoo. Otherwise, stay to the right at the fork as the road curves right. After about 1km you'll come upon two large barns on your right. Remember to keep scanning the fields and trees as you proceed — uncommon species such as dark-billed cuckoo and gray kingbird have been recorded at the Agricultural Research Station. About 250m beyond the barns you'll arrive at a four-way intersection. To the right is the derelict road you explored earlier on foot from the other end. To the left a road proceeds about 1km through more scrub and pasture; good unobstructed views make this another promising spot to search for the ventriloquial striped cuckoo (often seen perched atop fenceposts or shrubs).

If you proceed straight at this intersection, you'll arrive at a T intersection after about 400m. Turn right and proceed past more barns (on your left) and muddy cattle-holding areas (also on your left) that may yield some hitherto-unobserved shorebirds. After about 1km you'll arrive back at the bend where you began your circuit. By this stage you should've added many new species to your checklist. Proceed past the guard hut and retrace your route back to the Eastern Main Road.

ARENA FOREST
40km, 1 day

The Arena Forest is a lowland rainforest located in north-central Trinidad. The word *"arena"* refers to sand, the predominant soil type. The terrain averages 50m above sea level and is gently rolling, in sharp contrast to the nearly vertical terrain of the Northern Range. Located in this forest are the Arena Dam and Reservoir; a permit is required for each person entering the vicinity of the dam. You can obtain these permits from the Water and Sewerage Authority (WASA), Farm Road, St. Joseph, Trinidad, for about TT$5.50 each. Species to be seen on this trip include raptors, trogons, woodpeckers, woodcreepers, manakins, tanagers, hermit hummingbirds, and many insectivorous and ant-associating species.

To reach the Arena Forest, follow the Churchill-Roosevelt Highway east to Tumpuna Road (south of the town of Arima). Look for the blue-and-white "Arena Dam" sign on the left just before this traffic-light-controlled intersection.

Once on Tumpuna Road, bear right at 2.1km where the road curves sharply, cross a steel bridge over the Caroni River at 3.1km, and enter the village of San Rafael. You'll see a statue of St. Rafael on the right and a church on the left at 4.2km. Turn left at the T intersection and proceed for 1.1km, where the road curves to the right at an intersection. Stay right — you're now on Arena Road, which leads to the Arena forest and dam. The road deteriorates as you reach some small chicken farms 0.9km farther on, where the forest and good birding begin.

After driving another 0.5km, park and bird as far as you wish along a trail that leads to the left into the forest, looking and listening for little tinamou; plumbeous kite; white hawk; blue-headed

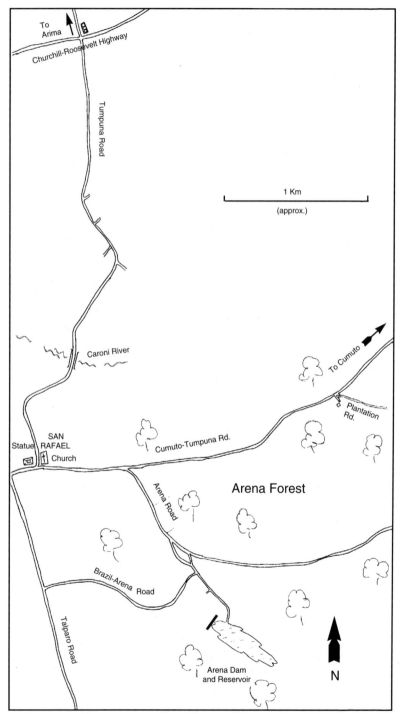

64   *Vicinity of the Arena Forest, Arena Dam, and Arena Reservoir in central Trinidad.*

Mud flats and brush edge surrounding the Arena Reservoir in central Trinidad.

parrot; blue-crowned motmot; trogons; channel-billed toucan; lineated, red-rumped, and golden-olive woodpeckers; woodcreepers; pale-breasted and stripe-breasted spinetails; great, barred, and black-crested antshrikes; black-tailed tityra; white-bellied antbird; rufous-tailed jacamar; little and striped cuckoos; hermits and other hummingbirds; white-bearded and golden-headed manakins; and the usual forest species.

Returning to your car, drive another 0.5km, at which point you'll see a trail on the left that leads into an open, scrubby area. Walk in and scan for raptors, especially plumbeous kite, and look among the brush and grass for sooty grassquit and ruddy-breasted and yellow-bellied seedeaters. In another 100m the road forks. Stay right and proceed to a T intersection after about 0.3km. Turn right and carefully note this spot for your return trip. Ignore a side road on the right after 100m and another at 0.8km. At the top of an uphill stretch (0.2km), present your pass(es) to the WASA officer and proceed to the area of the dam. (The dam was completed in the 1980s and does not yet appear on all roadmaps of Trinidad.)

Bear to the right and park in the parking lot next to the warden's house. To the left are the reservoir and the Central Range in the distance; to the right you can see the Northern Range. You'll see the dam wall straight ahead. Walk across the dam scanning both the reservoir and spillway for least and pied-billed grebes;

neotropic cormorant; anhinga; little blue and cocoi herons; great egret; black-bellied and fulvous whistling-ducks; osprey; swallow-tailed and plumbeous kites; common black-hawk; gray hawk; peregrine falcon; yellow-headed caracara; common moorhen; black-bellied plover; laughing gull; large-billed and yellow-billed terns; black skimmer; and southern rough-winged, barn, and white-winged swallows. The reservoir is so new that additional species are still discovering it, so your chances are good of turning up a real rarity here. Turn around at the end of the dam and return to your car.

Proceed back toward the gate but bear right, toward the reservoir. Park next to a small picnic and play area on the right. You'll be pleased to know that there are public lavatories here. Walk along the narrow footpath out to a concrete shelter at the end of the peninsula. Bird as you walk, paying attention to the nearby trees, grasses, and to the water's edge as well as to the distant shoreline for the species mentioned above as well as for green and striated herons; white-headed marsh-tyrant; pied water-tyrant; masked yellowthroat; green kingfisher; yellow-bellied elaenia; and piratic flycatcher. You should be able to find at least one of the many caimans that often bask along the water's edge. Return to your car when you've thoroughly scanned the area.

From the parking lot the road continues straight ahead and then turns left, then right, into a final picnic/play area. Feel free to bird these regions as well, paying attention to any coves you may see along the way on the right, as well as to the forest edges. From the final picnic area runs a narrow path (on the left as you leave the picnic area) that provides access to a site from which you can scan the reservoir from a different angle.

Retrace your route through the entrance gate and drive 1.0km, ignoring the two left turns, until you return to the intersection you noted on your way in. Turn right and proceed 100m to a T inter-section. Turn right and proceed along a narrow road that runs through the heart of the Arena Forest. Several productive forest trails begin on either side of the road. You may stop and bird as many of these as you wish. At a Y intersection after 1.8km, turn left and proceed 3.0km farther to the Cumuto-Tumpuna Road.

Turn left at this junction. If you wish to bird farther, look for the Arena Forest Reserve Rest House on the left after 2.2km; promi-nent Caribbean pines border the entranceway. Park on the entrance driveway and search the evergreens for ferruginous pygmy-owl and tropical screech-owl. Beyond a small shelter house beside the road you'll see the beginning of Plantation Road, which runs deep into the forest. When you're through, you may wish to carefully and quietly approach the abandoned building along the roadway. For several years a pair of common barn-owls have roosted in the upper rooms. When you're through exploring the area, turn left, back onto the Cumuto-Tumpuna Road, and proceed 2.5km to a T intersection that may look familiar — to the left is Areana Road, which you took on your way into the forest earlier. Turn right and proceed 1.1 km back to the intersection in San Rafael village (with church and statue). Turn right and retrace your earlier route 4.2km back to the Churchill-Roosevelt Highway.

MOUNT ST. BENEDICT AND ST. MICHEAL [sic]
15km, half day

The Mount St. Benedict/St. Micheal areas comprise a number of different habitats including open grasslands, tropical pine forest, and semi-cultivated, primary, and secondary forests. There are numerous good vantage points, making this a fine area for observing raptors and swifts. Birdlife to be found here includes hepatic tanager; southern beardless-tyrannulet; little tinamou; common black-, white, short-tailed, white-tailed, and zone-tailed hawks; ornate hawk-eagle; yellow-headed caracara; bat falcon; pale-vented pigeon; white-tipped dove; ferruginous pygmy-, spectacled, and tropical screech-owls; pauraque; rufous nightjar; squirrel and striped cuckoos; blue-tailed emerald; tufted coquette; green hermit; rufous-browed peppershrike; giant and shiny cowbirds; grayish saltator; yellow oriole; boat-billed, piratic, and streaked flycatchers; bright-rumped attila; sooty grassquit; chestnut-collared and lesser swallow-tailed swifts; fork-tailed palm-swift; streaked xenops; golden-headed manakin; and the usual species.

To reach Mount St. Benedict, follow the Eastern Main Road to Tunapuna, which is located about 20km east of Port-of-Spain. Turn north, toward the mountains, off the Eastern Main Road in Tunapuna, onto St. John's Road, which is just east of the Scarlet Ibis Hotel. [If you're thirsty, stop for a quick one at Tony's Pub on the left; tell them Bill says hello.]

Follow St. John's Road uphill, ignoring the numerous side roads and alleys. Proceed past St. John the Baptist Roman Catholic Church on the right at 1.0km. Bear right at the Y intersection at 1.2km. Proceed past an elementary school on the right shortly after this intersection, at 1.4km. Slow almost to a stop as you cross over two well-marked road humps (locally called "sleeping policemen"). Ignore a potential downhill right at 1.6km as you proceed uphill to the intersection of St. John's Road, St. Micheal Road, and

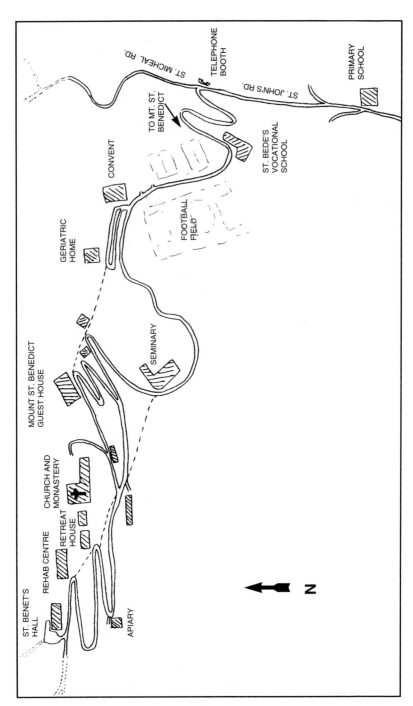

Mount St. Benedict / Tunapuna area, Trinidad.

the entrance drive to the Mount St. Benedict complex at 1.9km. A telephone booth on the right confirms your arrival here.

The lower reaches of this area, consisting of relatively dry foothills of no great elevation, are commonly known as St. Micheal. As squatters continue to practice slash-and-burn agriculture in the government-owned forests, the best birding areas are being pushed farther and farther up the valleys.

Many of the inhabitants of the St. Micheal area belong to the Rastafarian religious sect. The men are festooned with long braids ("dreadlocks") and are somewhat alarming in appearance. They are peaceful in demeanor, however, and mutual respect is called for in any encounters you might have with them.

To bird the St. Micheal area, proceed right at the "telephone booth" intersection mentioned above, onto St. Micheal Road. Continue past a large water storage tank on the right and stay to the right when the road forks shortly after this a 0.4km. Ignore a potential uphill left at 0.6km. From here on, the road deteriorates. You may wish to park on the side of the road here, making sure to leave room for other vehicles to get by, and proceed to a Y intersection at 0.8km. At this point you have two options, each involving the same two trails that are actually part of one loop:

1) If you proceed *left* at the Y intersection, you'll arrive at a left hairpin turn after approximately 120m. The bend continues to an old wooden cocoa-house. From the bend, a small trail leads through a semi-cultivated estate and into the forest beyond.

2) If you proceed *right* at the Y intersection you'll arrive at a small stream after about 90m. A trail begins here and leads into the forest.

To visit or bird the Mount St. Benedict area, follow the directions above to the three-way intersection at the telephone booth. Instead of turning right, onto St. Micheal Road, turn sharply left and head uphill. During daylight hours, simply pass through the security gate; after dark, explain to the guard in attendance the nature of your visit. Two switchbacks beyond the gate, you'll drive past the St. Bede Vocational School and a playing field, both on the left. Follow the road along the perimeter of this field, ignoring any roads on the right, unless your plans include a visit to a convent or a geriatric home. Proceed past the Regional Seminary on the right, and after the next left switchback, at 1.0km, look for a small sign that says "PAX Guest House" (a.k.a. Pax Guest House Mount St. Benedict) on an inconspicuous right switchback from the main road. This drive will take you through three switchbacks to the parking lot of the guest house. If you accidentally miss this turnoff in your haste, don't worry — about 250m farther on you can make a hairpin right turn at a sign on the left that says "Apiary, Retreat House, Rehab Center." This road also will take you to the guest house. Turn hard right, stay to the right past a Y intersection, and proceed about 200m over the slight hill and around the bend to the guest house on the left.

Even if you're staying elsewhere, feel free to say hello to the manager at the guest house, Mr. Gerard Ramsawak. Gerard is a keen birder who will be able to offer advice and answer any questions you may have. The parking lot is a great area for viewing swifts, raptors, parrots, and parrotlets. Nearby vegetation may yield chivi vireo; golden-fronted greenlet; long-billed gnatwren; yellow-breasted flycatcher; great and barred antshrikes; and white-tailed and violaceous trogons, as well as the usual species.

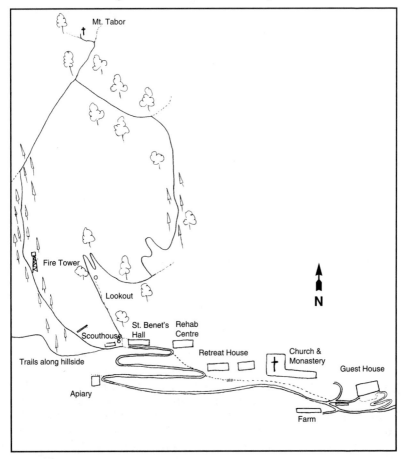

70   *Trails above St. Benet's Hall, Mount St. Benedict, Trinidad.*

To bird the higher reaches of Mount St. Benedict, return to the "Apiary, Retreat House, Rehab Center" sign just up the hill from the guest house. Keep your eyes open for streaked flycatcher, long-billed starthroat, and blue-tailed emerald, which nest in this area, and for gray-headed kite and zone-tailed hawk, which patrol the slopes below. Continue your ascent by proceeding straight ahead. Make a right hairpin turn (the apiary is located on this corner), a left hairpin turn (avoiding the archway that leads to the retreat house and monastery), another right hairpin turn (overlooking the apiary), and a final left hairpin turn at 0.4km in front of the Rehab Center, which leads you uphill to the parking lot of St. Benet's Hall. The road continues and ends slightly farther uphill next to a long building, a scout house/craft shop, which marks the beginning of the western approach to the trail. If you're staying at the guest house, I'd recommend that you walk the route outlined, scanning the fields, trees, and shrubbery along the way and looking overhead for raptors, even though you can follow a footpath from the road in front of the Guest House to St. Benet's Hall.

From the St. Benet's Hall parking lot you're ready to explore the forest on foot. Watch for woodcreepers; woodpeckers; white-tipped dove; golden-headed manakin; ochre-bellied flycatcher; little tinamou; little, rufous-breasted, and green hermits; white-tailed and violaceous trogons; and the usual forest species.

The trail is actually a circuit loop and can thus be walked from either the east or the west. The western approach is very steep; we therefore suggest that you tackle this trail from the eastern side, which begins in the parking lot proper, to make the more difficult section downhill rather than uphill. To start, look for the trail head, which begins below two water tanks at the western end of the concrete wall.

Proceed along this trail, sharply downhill at first, birding as you go. After 170m you'll arrive at a 30-m-long steel footbridge clinging to the cliffside. The bridge affords an excellent view across the forest canopy and over the ravine below to the opposite ridge. About 50m beyond the bridge, the trail forks. Keep left (uphill). After about 160m you'll cross the headwaters of a small stream as the trail switches back to the right, followed by a left switchback and another right switchback. Continue through the forest for about 250m, where you'll arrive at an inconspicuous intersection. Take the sharp left here and follow this route for about 350m into a more open area with tall grass, shrubs, and Caribbean pines. From here you can catch glimpses of the Plains of Caroni to the southeast. You're now on a side ridge that leads up to the main ridge. After about 360m you'll arrive at another inconspicuous junction;

turn left, and after 280m you'll arrive at a prominent intersection that marks your arrival at the main ridge. Here you have two options:

1) If you wish to go still higher to bird Mount Tabor, turn right at this intersection and after 180m make a sharp left. In another 60m, you'll find the weatherworn remains of the original monastery on a small hillock to the right.

2) If you wish to proceed along the main ridge, turn left. After about 200m you'll arrive at an open area with many ferns and large quartz boulders. Here you'll have spectacular views into the Maracas Valley (to your right) and down past the monastery complex onto the Plains of Caroni (to your left). This area is as good as it gets for raptor watching. Find some shade among the pines just ahead and scan Maracas Valley for any birds of prey that may be rising on thermals. Patience usually pays off here. After about another 150m you'll reach a rustic bench. At this point the trail turns left and begins a sharp descent through a grove of Caribbean pines that were transplanted to here from their native island of Hispaniola. If you follow this steep section for 350m, you'll arrive at a fire tower. Watch out, though — this trek may be quite slippery and tough on the knees. If you're not afraid of heights, the fire tower would be another good place from which to look for raptors and swifts. A further 250m below the tower is a large reflector board on the left. About 50m beyond that you'll see the long building (scout house/craft shop) just above the St. Benet's Hall parking lot, where you started your hike.

Another productive trail begins at the western end of the scout house (under the large forestry sign). This trail skirts westward along the southern face of the hillside for several hundred meters through vegetation consisting of Caribbean pines, scrub, and tall grass. The area is good for sooty grassquit; long-billed starthroat; streaked xenops; plain-brown and buff-throated woodcreepers; lineated and golden-olive woodpeckers; rufous-breasted wren; and the usual species.

WALLERFIELD AND ARIPO SAVANNAH
20km, half day

The area southeast of Arima contains one of the last remaining natural savannahs in Trinidad. Birding can be very productive here throughout the year. Two areas of particular interest are Wallerfield and the Aripo Savannah. Wallerfield is an abandoned U.S. airbase that dates back to World War II. It consists of two east-west runways serviced by a network of old roads. Except for the

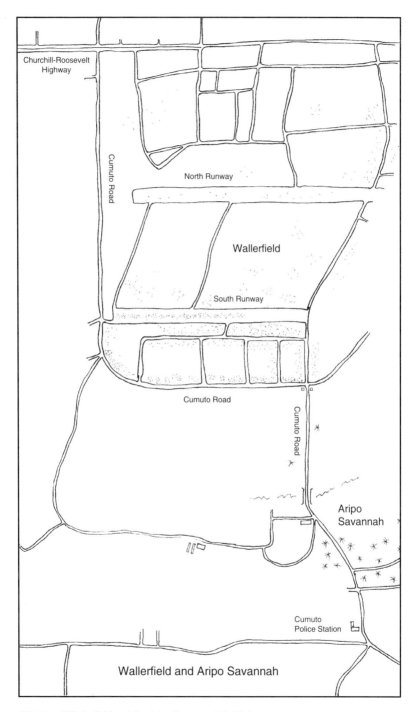

Vicinity of Wallerfield and the Aripo Savanna, Trinidad.

Seedeater and grassquit habitat. Shrubs and grass along south runway at Wallerfield, Trinidad.

sterile concrete runways and roads, the area is overgrown with trees, brush, and grass.

The Aripo Savannah is a seasonally wet prairie with a unique assemblage of trees and plants. You can see about 70 species of birds in the region, including pearl, gray-headed, and hook-billed kites; gray hawk; savanna hawk; yellow-headed caracara; red-bellied macaw; striped cuckoo; ruby-topaz hummingbird; fork-tailed palm-swift; sulphury and bran-colored flycatchers; lesser elaenia; southern beardless-tyrannulet; yellow-rumped cacique; and the extremely rare moriche oriole. It's also one of the most reliable spots in Trinidad for glimpsing mongoose.

To reach Wallerfield, drive east from Arima on the Churchill-Roosevelt Highway. Pass between two stone pillars that mark the beginning of a dual carriageway (and the boundary of the former U.S. Army base called Fort Reid). Proceed for about 3.5km, where you'll arrive at a 4-way intersection. Look carefully for this intersection since it's relatively unmarked. Turn right onto Cumuto Road.

Follow Cumuto Road as it veers sharply left after 2km. At 3.7km you'll come to a sharp right-hand bend. Instead of following this bend, turn sharply left and park. This is the south entrance to

Wallerfield. You should see a sign on the right saying "Wallerfield Racing Circuit. du Maurier Supercircuit Championship Competitors Entrance" (the south runway is used for auto racing). The cattle pasture behind you often holds southern lapwing, wattled jacana, and an occasional savanna hawk or yellow-headed caracara. Ahead of you is the south runway of Wallerfield. The vegetation on either side of this short road is good for hermit hummingbirds and other hummingbirds; barred and black-crested antshrikes; rufous-tailed jacamar; blue-crowned motmot; turquoise and white-shouldered tanagers; blue dacnis; bran-colored flycatcher; and southern rough-winged and white-winged swallows.

About 50m along this entrance road, on the left, is an inconspicuous road that connects with a network of roads south of the runway. Look here for black-tailed tityra; squirrel cuckoo; rufous-tailed jacamar; hook-billed kite (rather sedentary); black-crested antshrike; yellow-breasted flycatcher; and black-throated mango. After about 0.5km you'll reach a short connecting road on the right that leads to the south runway.

Drive and walk as much of the Wallerfield area as you wish, exploring all of the areas accessible by road. Huge flocks of black vultures roost on the runways. Zone-tailed hawks mimic turkey vultures overhead, and at times as many as three hook-billed kites have been seen at one time. In the rainy season, flooded areas sometimes develop that attract such species as wattled jacana; white-headed marsh-tyrant; pied water-tyrant; southern lapwing; and yellow-chinned spinetail. In the evening this is a good spot to use a flashlight to look for the reflected light in the eyes of pauraques and white-tailed nightjars and to try for the rare Nacunda nighthawk. After dark, the still-warm concrete surfaces at Wallerfield host hundreds of nightjars and pauraques. Common barn-owl and common potoo can sometimes be heard or seen overhead or in nearby bushes.

(A note of caution is in order here. Wallerfield is an isolated area away from main thoroughfares. You'd be wise not to attract too much attention. Stay close to your car at all times. Night birding here is advised only if you're part of a larger group.)

When you've finished birding Wallerfield, return to the access road where you entered and continue south on Cumuto Road, immediately passing between an old pair of stone posts that used to mark the southern entrance to the airbase. Cross the muddy Aripo River via a steel bridge at 0.9km and continue around a left bend. At 1.3km, turn sharply right so that a large derelict building is now on your left. Pay attention to the fields, bushes, and treetops on the right for such species as rufous-tailed jacamar, southern lapwing, 75

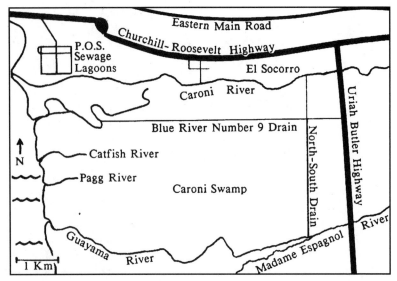

Caroni area showing locations of El Socorro marsh, Caroni Swamp, and Port-of-Spain sewage lagoons in Trinidad.

giant cowbird, common snipe, and plumbeous kite. Proceed 0.4km and turn left at a T intersection. The enormous slate-colored animals grazing in the nearby field are water buffalo. Proceed another 0.3km, carefully scanning the pasture, distant trees, and sky for savanna hawk, fork-tailed palm-swift, green-rumped parrotlet, yellow-headed caracara, peregrine falcon, black-crested antshrike, and fork-tailed flycatcher.

Follow the road as it veers right and proceed 0.4km past some small chicken farms on the left. Just beyond these is an open grassy area on the left. This is a good place to stop and search for striped cuckoo, ruby-topaz hummingbird, sulphury flycatcher, and white-flanked antwren. You can proceed farther along this road, birding as you go, although it becomes more closed in.

Retrace your route to Cumuto Road and turn right (not hard right onto the small lane). Moriche palms, actually a type of palmetto, are soon visible on both sides of the road. At 0.5km look on the left for an obscure dirt lane that penetrates deep into the Aripo Savannah. The savannah itself is a fragile community and the government has designated it a restricted area; therefore, you mustn't venture off the lane. Drive into the savannah, or walk if the path is muddy, birding the shrubs and palms for fork-tailed palm-swift, ruby-topaz hummingbird, lesser elaenia, red-bellied macaw, sulphury flycatcher, and moriche oriole. Except for the palm-swift, finding these species requires keen powers of observation. As always, patience pays off.

Boat trip exploring the Blue River in the Caroni Swamp. Best place inTrinidad for scarlet ibis, bicolored conebill, greater ani, and other mangrove-loving species.

Retrace your route to Cumuto Road, turn left, drive 0.6km, turn right, and park at the Cumuto Police Station/Health Center with its longstanding colony of yellow-rumped caciques in the Caribbean pines. During the week, the restroom facilities at the Health Center are available upon request. At LC's store across the street, for years Lenore Noray and her family have offered shade, cold drinks, tasty food, and a friendly reception to birders. Pay her a visit, say "Hey!" to the kids, and treat yourself to a snack.

To return to the Churchill-Roosevelt Highway, retrace Cumuto Road for 6km.

WETLANDS

CARONI SWAMP
10km, half day

A *"must visit"* destination for every naturalist visiting Trinidad is an evening excursion into the Caroni Swamp. A spectacular event is the homecoming flight of egrets, herons, and scarlet ibis. The flight begins between 4:00 and 5:00 p.m. and continues until after sunset. These large waders roost communally on mangrove hammocks, with the scarlet ibis — the stars of the show — forming the upper tier and the herons and egrets settling mostly in the lower branches. The sight of vivid hues of red and white set against a backdrop of dark green foliage at sunset is an unforgettable visual treat as the mangrove islands gradually assume the appearance of decorated Christmas trees.

The Caroni Swamp Bird Sanctuary is located 20 minutes south of Port-of-Spain and extends approximately 25km along Trinidad's western shoreline. The swamp proper is approximately 40 square miles in size and was created by land depression south of the Northern Range. The government has set aside about 450 acres within the swamp as the Caroni Swamp Bird Sanctuary. The entrance is accessible from the Uriah Butler Highway, which forms the eastern boundary of the Caroni Swamp. Specific directions follow later in this section.

The entire Caroni area is tidal, with a difference of about 1m between high and low tides. Because of the climatic conditions of the tropics, the area is influenced to a great extent by the intrusion of copious quantities of fresh water from the interior — particularly during the wet season, which normally extends from May through November. The mixture of fresh and salt water creates the brackish water condition that's so crucial to the diversity of the Caroni's flora and fauna.

The vegetation within the Caroni Swamp can be described in general as "mangrove"; the term isn't a taxonomic classification and thus may be used to cover all vegetation found in the intertidal zone or substrate. However, the Caroni is dominated by a single species of rhyzophore, commonly called "red mangrove." This type of mangrove ecosystem is the reason why animal life abounds in Caroni. It serves as the foundation a complex food chain that attracts and supports the wide variety of wading and other kinds of birds. In sum, birders have recorded more than 185 species of birds from the Caroni Swamp.

To reach the Caroni Swamp Bird Sanctuary, begin at the intersection of the Churchill-Roosevelt and Uriah Butler (formerly the Princess Margaret) Highways. Drive south 5.0km to a sign that says "Caroni Bird Sanctuary." Follow the signs, crossing the overpass and descending on a feeder road that runs along the right side of the highway. Turn left and park just beyond the propane tank refilling station, where you see the boats docked. The boat tours leave from the south side of the channel, the technical name of which is Blue River Drain Number 9.

Very important — before embarking on a boat trip into the Caroni Swamp, verify that your boatman is familiar with the specialty birds of the mangroves and will endeavor to show you not only the scarlet ibis but also species you have little chance to see elsewhere: boat-billed heron and common potoo (nocturnal), dark-billed and mangrove cuckoos, greater ani, green-throated mango, straight-billed woodcreeper, bicolored conebill, and red-capped cardinal. At times boatloads of tourists originating from cruise ships docked in Port-of-Spain visit Caroni Swamp. Your inclusion in such an eclectic group will be a bitter disappointment to you because your boatman will merely transport the chattering crowd to and from the scarlet ibis roost. Professional birding guides, on the other hand, pilot the boat to prime areas in response to specific requests from birders. They also pack strong lanterns with which they search out and illuminate boat-billed herons and common potoos after dark.

Before departing by boat for the scarlet ibis roost, consider spending some time birding the area on foot. Many species of birds found only with great difficulty elsewhere in Trinidad are found easily inthe mangroves bordering the channels. Species to look for include pied-billed grebe; neotropic cormorant; anhinga; pinnated, stripe-backed, and least bitterns; all of the common egrets and herons; the rarely seen rufescent tiger-heron; boat-billed heron; roseate spoonbill; fulvous and black-bellied whistling-ducks; masked duck; merlin; peregrine falcon; long-winged harrier (rare); aplomado falcon (rare); yellow-headed caracara; sora; common moorhen; purple gallinule; limpkin; large-billed tern; a wide variety of shorebirds; dark-billed and mangrove cuckoos; greater ani; common potoo; green-throated mango; straight-billed woodcreeper; yellow-chinned spinetail; fork-tailed flycatcher; migrant North American warblers, primarily American redstart and northern waterthrush; bicolored conebill; and red-capped cardinal.

During the wet season a pair of wading boots comes in handy for the walk along the channel, as the trail is sometimes covered by a few inches of water. Begin your hike by walking along the south side of the channel. At the west end of the boat dock, a trail leads to the left between a freshwater marsh on the left and a brackish marsh on the right, both good for rails, crakes, and bitterns. Another trail leads straight ahead along the river to the edge of a shallow lake, good for ducks, shorebirds, herons, egrets, terns, and osprey. Watch for small flocks of chattering green-rumped parrotlets darting through the riverside mangroves. Birders often find resting tree boas (*Corallus enydris*) balled-up among the outermost twigs of the mangroves. This species isn't docile and can attain a length of six feet, so look but don't touch. Be sure to return to the boat dock in plenty of time for the boat trip's scheduled departure.

While birding along the channel, whether on foot or in a boat, scan the water's surface occasionally for four-eyed fish (*Anableps*). These unique creatures actually have only two eyes, divided into upper and lower halves, each half with its own focal length, endowing *Anableps* with simultaneous dual vision. Schools of these fish glide smoothly along just beneath the surface, the upper pupils protruding above water scanning for predators, the lower pupils scanning the aquatic world for morsels on which to feed. You should be able to observe at least one school of *Anableps* during your visit.

EL SOCORRO MARSH
10km, half day

[Channelization of the Caroni River began draining El Socorro Marsh in the late 1980s, driving out resident and migrant species of birds. In past years, sugarcane and vegetable fields planted around the perimeter of the marsh were flooded periodically because of siltation of the Caroni River, a result of clearcutting and poor land management in the upstream watershed. The description given here is provided in hopes that conservationists can step in before the marsh is drained completely.]

El Socorro Marsh has traditionally been one of the best places in Trinidad to observe a wide variety of unusual and often difficult-to-find species of birds such as white-faced whistling-duck, masked duck, rufous-necked wood-rail, sora, ash-throated and yellow-breasted crake, spotted rail, and the tiny crested doradito, as well as more common species such as yellow-chinned spinetail. The marsh is located north of the Caroni River, south of the major roads and east of Port-of-Spain. Unlike the brackish Caroni Swamp just to the south, El Socorro is a freshwater marsh with vegetation that consists of rushes, sedges, and a few woody shrubs. You can bird the marsh from adjacent roads and lanes, but to see the greatest number of species, don a pair of boots and explore the marsh on its own terms. Watch carefully for protectively camouflaged, "frozen" bitterns and for rails that skulk away upon your approach.

To reach El Socorro Marsh, proceed west (toward Port-of-Spain) on the Churchill-Roosevelt Highway from the stoplight at the Uriah Butler Highway. In 0.9km, after passing a vast expanse of vegetable fields on the left, turn left onto Chootoo Road into a suburban housing tract. Follow the road as it bends sharply to the right. Turn left at the sign for Zolaz mufflers on the left and follow the road a short distance to its end at the marsh. Park and walk out along a dike into the marsh, looking and listening for large-billed tern, yellow-chinned spinetail, ruddy-breasted seedeater, and yellow-hooded and red-breasted blackbirds. You can walk the marsh east for about 1.5km to the San Juan River, south 0.5km to

Mesic woodland along Depot Trace near North Manzanilla, Trinidad.

the Caroni River, or west about 1.5km to the heavily forested eastern edge of the Port-of-Spain landfill and sewage lagoons. Watch for pearl kite on the overhead wires.

If you prefer to drive rather than walk, continue west toward Port-of-Spain along the streets closest to the marsh, making jaunts to their south ends at the edge of El Socorro Marsh, birding from the dead ends. Loud, raucous cries, whistles, and groans that emanate from the vicinity of the marsh are often produced by caged macaws and parrots in the yards of the houses that border the marsh. Many of the other avian sounds are produced by smooth-billed anis, which are common in the brush. Still other calls are produced by a number of different species of skulking marsh birds such as sora and yellow-breasted crake (both abundant), spotted rail (common), and rufous-necked wood-rail and ash-throated crake (both very rare). You can use a portable tape recorder very effectively when birding El Socorro Marsh to lure these secretive species into view.

NARIVA SWAMP AND EASTERN TRINIDAD
80km, 1 day

Birders visiting eastern Trinidad can explore a great variety of habitats in one all-day trip. The excursion described here covers

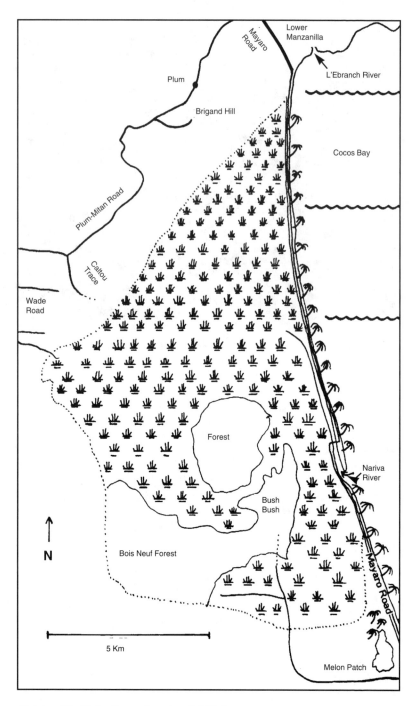

Vicinity of the Nariva Swamp in eastern Trinidad.

the most productive birding spots — Brigand Hill, Plum Mitan Road, Manzanilla Beach/Mayaro Road, Bush Bush Creek, Nariva Swamp, the Melon Patch, and Point Radix.

Brigand Hill, the easternmost peak of the Central Range, will provide you with an unforgettable panoramic view of most of eastern Trinidad as well as good birding in a region of semi-abandoned cocoa plantations and uninhabited rainforest. If you wish to bird Brigand Hill, you might save some driving by telephoning or visiting the Forestry Division office in Sangre Grande to determine if the Brigand Hill station is open (ask your hotel manager for the current telephone number and location in Sangre Grande).

The Nariva Swamp occupies a vast triangular area along the eastern coast of Trinidad, from the village of Lower Manzanilla in the north almost to Point Radix in the south, and as far inland as the Central Range. Freshwater habitat predominates, except for brackish mangrove edges along the Nariva River and Bush Bush Creek, and provides excellent habitat for waders, rails, raptors, and at least one large aquatic mammal, the manatee. A walk along the banks of Bush Bush Creek may yield black-crested antshrike, silvered antbird, green-throated mango, green kingfisher, limpkin, white-tailed kite, and gray hawk. In Nariva Swamp proper, red-bellied macaws and waders, both large and small, are the main attractions. Finally, Point Radix offers spectacular views along the coconut-palm-fringed coast and close — often much too close — views of black vultures.

Brigand Hill area. Coffee trees along Maridale Road in eastern Trinidad. 83

To reach eastern Trinidad, follow the Eastern Main Road past Valencia and then through Sangre Grande, the largest city in eastern Trinidad. Continue to the town of Upper Manzanilla. Immediately beyond a large wooden store on the left, turn left onto North Manzanilla Road. Drive for 3.6km, then turn right onto Depot Trace, which descends into an unusually dry littoral forest. Bird the next 0.6km on foot to the end of the trace, near a tidal pool, across which you can see the fishing hamlet of

Brigand Hill area. Rainforest along LaVictoria Road.

North Manzanilla. This short stretch of road sometimes is productive for some of the inconspicuous and less common insectivorous species such as olive-striped flycatcher and short-tailed pygmy-tyrant.

Return to the Eastern Main Road, turn left (south), and drive 0.5km, crossing the bridge over the L'Ebranche River. You'll soon arrive at a very wide T intersection. Turn right onto Plum Mitan Road. Drive 2.8km, bearing left at the Y intersection. At 3.5km, a hard left will put you on an 0.8-km-long, very steep but well paved road that climbs to the lighthouse atop Brigand Hill. If your vehicle can handle the grade, drive to the top, park, and tell the guard that you're birdwatching. If you question your car's ability to climb the hill, park, walk up the hill, and tell the guard that you're birdwatching. This is one of the steepest roads anywhere, and you should be careful not to overexert yourself. Consider stopping

Coconut palms along Cocos Bay, Nariva area, eastern Trinidad. Good for brown noddy, brown pelican, occasional shearwaters and petrels.

occasionally to bird, if only to afford yourself a dignified excuse to catch your breath.

The Brigand Hill light station is an automatic apparatus situated atop open steel scaffolding. Walk up the incline to the lighthouse and climb the stairs as high as you feel comfortable. You'll be rewarded with extensive views to the southeast of the entire Nariva Swamp area and beyond, a good view to the northeast past the satellite-tracking radiotelescope dish at Matura at the eastern end of the Northern Range, and a reasonably good view to the west along the spine of the Central Range. On the southeastern horizon you may be able to discern a fiery column of burning gas jetting from Texaco's offshore oil platform 70km out in the Atlantic and an even more distant jet in the Galeota oilfield. To spot these objects, sight out to sea just over the tip of Point Radix, the cliff-sided headland to the southeast.

From the Brigand Hill lighthouse you can see more than one million coconut palms at one time. The coconut palms are grown in

Mangroves along Bush Bush Creek, good for silvered antbird.

plantations along Mayaro Road, the thin strand of asphalt that runs parallel to Cocos Bay on a narrow strand of high, sandy ground that separates Nariva Swamp from the Atlantic. A large flock of black vultures usually mans the base of the lighthouse and can be approached closely. You can also view several species of swifts advantageously from the tower.

After relishing the terrific view from Brigand Hill, bird your way back down to Plum Mitan Road, stopping at each switchback to bird. Look among the abundant heliconias for eight species of hummingbirds, including all three species of hermit humming-birds, and overhead for tanagers, euphonias, elaenias, flycatchers, trogons, and others. This area is both unusually birdy because of the tremendous numbers of insects that are attracted to the light and unusually easy to bird because the steepness of the road allows eye-level views of canopy-loving species.

Again on Plum Mitan Road, turn left almost immediately onto Maridale Road, which follows the contours of Brigand Hill east along its base. Excellent birding is possible in this verdant rain-forest. Canopy-loving species and hermit hummingbirds are par-ticularly abundant. The uncommon crimson-crested woodpecker is often found here as well. Formerly a cocoa plantation, this area has been allowed to return to a more diversified state. Bird for 1.5km, then turn around at the house at the end of the road and return to Plum Mitan Road.

Turn left on Plum Mitan Road, drive 0.2km, and turn right onto LaVictoria Road. The vegetation along this 1.2-km-long road is similar to that along Maridale Road, but the area is slightly drier. The major difference between the two roads is that Maridale Road heads east, whereas LaVictoria Road heads west, so depending upon the time of day during which you bird this area, visibility into the canopy will be far more favorable on one road than on the other. I tend to bird along Maridale Road in the morning and along LaVictoria Road in the afternoon.

To continue your trip toward the ocean, return to Plum Mitan Road, turn left, and retrace your route 5.0km back to its intersection with the Eastern Main Road. Cross the intersection and proceed east on Mayaro Road. [Consider this point to be 0.0km in the following directions.] Food and drink are available at the Chrystal [sic] Restaurant (6.4km), just before Mayaro Road drops steeply down to the seacoast along Cocos Bay. In the next 25km you'll pass those million coconut palms, growing on both sides of the road. The narrow strip of sand on which the road was built and on which the palms grow was perhaps a former barrier island.

Wherever possible, pull out and park along the beach. Scan the usually heavy surf for brown pelican, terns, and Leach's storm-petrel. This beach has produced most of Trinidad's petrel and shearwater records, mostly exhausted, ill, or dead birds.

View to the east along Point Radix. Overlook for brown noddy, brown pelican, and common black-hawk.

On the right at
9.6km you'll note
a dense grove of
mangroves, which
provides a perfect
habitat for a number
of specialized bird
species, including
silvered antbird
and bicolored
conebill. The man-
grove edge
is accessible for
the next 9km and
should be checked
well, although in
wet weather a

shallow depression between the road and the mangroves fills with
rainwater and makes birding more difficult. At 14.6km you'll pass
a copra-processing plant (all hand labor) and small huts that house
the workers.

At 18.0km, you may wish to take the sandy track on the left, just at
the bend in the road. A short drive will take you to the tip of a
peninsula formed by the junction of the Nariva River and the
Atlantic. Be careful not to drive in deep sand; tow trucks are hard
to come by in eastern Trinidad. Along the oceanside near the
mouth of the Nariva River look for resting shorebirds, terns, and
black skimmers.

Back on the main road, or still on the main road if you chose not to
drive to the tip, park at the Nariva River bridge. Walk out onto the
bridge and scan the mangroves for limpkins, anhingas, and herons.

At 19.6km, park just after crossing the bridge over the stream,
which is the legendary Bush Bush Creek of C. Brooke Worth fame
(author of **A Naturalist in Trinidad**). Bird along the swamp edge,
clambering on the intertwined mangrove roots if you like. This is
the best place in all of Trinidad to spot silvered antbird. Just ahead,
the shoreline and transient sandbars at the mouth of the Nariva
River sometimes hold resting shorebirds, terns, and black
skimmers.

At 22.7km, you'll pass a water buffalo ranch on the right, where
the wet fields are productive for great blue and cocoi herons,
southern lapwing, wattled jacana, savanna hawk, and other more
common species. Be sure to scan all the trees and fenceposts for
raptors as this area has produced rufous crab-hawk, gray hawk,

pearl kite, gray-headed kite, common black-hawk, and yellow-headed caracara.

At 23.4km (white stone mile marker 48-3/4), note the field on the right, which contains "islands" of royal palms. Between 5:00 p.m. and dark, hundreds of red-bellied macaws fly in from neighboring areas to roost in these trees. The macaws land in the top fronds of the palms and slide slowly down into the foliage until they can no longer be seen. Be certain to visit this spot again at dusk.

At 24.1km, turn right onto a one-lane paved road, park, and bird the freshwater ponds on the right on foot. If you continue along this road, you very soon break out of the endless coconut palms into a vast, open area called the Melon Patch. This has been a fabulously productive marsh until recently. It yielded South America's first western reef-heron in January 1986 and, more recently, has hosted a small colony of azure gallinules. In the early 1990s this section of the Nariva Swamp was ditched, burned, cultivated for rice production, then allowed to revert back to a more wild state. Depending on the condition of the wetlands, you may find the birding either fascinating or forgettable. Usually you can find purple gallinules, wattled jacanas, yellow-hooded blackbirds, and a variety of raptors, such as yellow-headed caracara. The latter species is often pursued by the much smaller tropical kingbird.

The lesser roads and paths in this area lead into interior forests in which birds may be more abundant and tamer than in adjacent "mainland" forests. Bands of red howler and capuchin monkeys inhabit Bush Bush Forest and can best be heard in the hours around dawn. At least one pinnated bittern can usually be found by persistent scanning. Look for what appears as a buffy pointed post sticking out of the rice. If you stand dusk watch in the Melon Patch, you can watch 50-200 red-bellied macaws fly over you on their way to roost. Orange-winged parrots also will be flying past in the distance, providing ample opportunity to contrast the wing-beats and flight styles of these two psittiform birds. Other common fly-bys include great and snowy egrets and little blue herons. Any day now, some keen birder is going to identify and photograph a lesser yellow-headed vulture coursing low over this marsh.

Returning to the main road, turn right and continue along Mayaro Road. You'll soon cross a large steel bridge over the Ortoire River. At the far end of the bridge is the fishing village of Ortoire. Take the second left, which will take you out onto Point Radix. Bird as far as you can go, to the gate of a private estate. Along the way, pull off on the left at a conspicuous overlook. The view here is to the north. and encompasses those one million coconut palms you drove past earlier as well as several isolated rocks below, upon which rest brown pelicans and an occasional tern, including brown noddy.

If you wish to photograph black vultures at point-blank range, take the only right turn on your way back to Mayaro Road. You'll find yourself at the mouth of the Ortoire River, where black vultures gather and feed almost underfoot among the fishermen. Green and ringed kingfishers also may be seen along this stretch of river, but the constant trade winds off the ocean make most landbirding endeavors very difficult.

From Ortoire you can return from whence you came via Mayaro Road and the Eastern Main Road.

PIARCO WATER TREATMENT PLANT
1km, 1 hour

Just across the road from Piarco International Airport in north-central Trinidad is the Piarco Water Treatment Plant. A visit to this site immediately upon entering Trinidad can be a wonderful intro-duction to tropical birding. This little known but highly worth-while birding spot can yield a large number of interesting species. This is a terrific place for onward-bound passengers to spend time while awaiting their flight. Currently it's only open on weekdays.

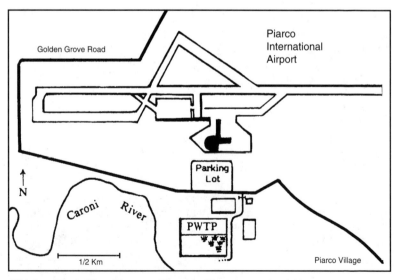

Vicinity of Piarco Water Treatment Plant near Piarco International Airport.

Bird-rich holding pond at Piarco Water Treatment Plant, across road from Piarco International Airport, Trinidad.

To visit the site, secure a permit in advance (see section on the Arena Forest for information on how to obtain the WASA permit).

To reach the Piarco Water Treatment Plant, turn left as you exit the airport; most traffic will be turning right, toward Port-of-Spain. Make the first possible right a short distance farther, just past the roadside food vendors, through a gate in the high wire fence. Stop at the gate and give your permit to the guards, who will allow you to enter and who will be glad to explain to you where you may or may not venture.

Park on the left just beyond the guardhouse. You'll be directed toward two ponds that lie beyond the main buildings. The sterile-looking pond nearer to the airport is usually unproductive, whereas the other pond is very birdy because of its emergent aquatic vegetation. Here you can find such species as white-headed marsh-tyrant, pied water-tyrant, wattled jacana, yellow-hooded and red-breasted blackbirds, southern lapwing, tropical kingbird, gray-breasted martin, white-winged swallow, anhinga, large-billed and yellow-billed terns, blue-black grassquit, yellow oriole, carib grackle, shiny and giant cowbirds, ruddy ground-dove, fork-tailed flycatcher, and at least one large reptile, the spectacled caiman.

Little direction is needed as to how to bird the ponds. Just walk the peripheries and you'll see all the wildlife. From about November through March, watch the skies for peregrine falcons and merlins, which frequent the sugarcane plantations in the near vicinity.

91

POINTE-À-PIERRE WILD FOWL TRUST
160km, half day

Who could imagine that 26 hectares within a large petrochemical complex could be attractive to birders? One naturalist did, and you can benefit from her foresight and perseverance. Ms. Molly Gaskin, Trinidad's most outspoken conservationist, established the Pointe-à-Pierre Wild Fowl Trust in 1966. Boasting two lakes and a profusion of native plants and trees, this exquisite compound near San Fernando on the central west coast of Trinidad is an interesting example of heavy industry and conservation working together.

The Trust is a national, nonprofit, volunteer organization dedicated to, and actively involved in the breeding of Trinidad's endangered species of waterfowl, cagebirds, and other indigenous species. The Trust also has initiated an environmental educational audiovisual program that's shown in schools and to community groups throughout Trinidad and Tobago. The Trust property is a wetland habitat, a peaceful haven where visitors may relax. It also serves as an environmental education resource center for scouts, guides, youth groups, and government ministries, providing out-of-classroom training and action projects. Visiting hours are 9:00 a.m. to 5:00 p.m. Monday through Friday and 10:00 a.m. to 6:00 p.m. on weekends.

The main building — the Learning Center — houses information dealing with living organisms and their habitats, a unique shell collection, and a small but comprehensive Amerindian museum.

Impoundments and adjoining areas host myriads of migrant waterfowl and shorebirds in the proper seasons. Other species can be seen throughout the year. Opportunities for close-up photography are excellent as the birds are accustomed to close approaches by humans. Species of particular interest include purple gallinule, anhinga, neotropic cormorant, white-winged becard, white-winged swallow, red-capped cardinal, sooty grassquit, slate-colored seedeater, and saffron finch. Among the captive species are black-bellied, fulvous, and white-faced whistling-ducks; Canada goose; mute and black-necked swans; white-cheeked and silver pintail; hooded merganser; Laysan, Brazilian, and blue-winged teal; common and paradise shelducks; mandarin, muscovy, wood, ring-necked, rosybill, and ruddy ducks; and red-crested pochard.

Persons interested in visiting the Trust are urged to make reservations and to secure detailed directions well in advance of their visit.

Mixed vegetation, Port-of-Spain sewage lagoons. Excellent for peregrine falcon, merlin, common black-hawk, rails, and shorebirds.

Address —   The Pointe-à-Pierre Wild Fowl Trust
                 c/o 42 Sandown Road
                 Goodwood Park
                 Point Cumana, Trinidad, W.I.
                 (809) 637-5145 or (809) 662-4040

PORT-OF-SPAIN SEWAGE LAGOONS
12km, half day

Can you imagine the reaction of a non-birder flipping through this book and spotting this heading? Sewage lagoons as a target destination on a birding trip to the tropics? This is something from a *Saturday Night Live* skit, right? Not! Although the name may be downright repulsive, the POS sewage lagoons are fabulously bird-rich and certainly deserving of a visit.

I'm not known to be a hardcore lister, one who purposefully sets out to amass the longest possible list of bird species seen on a trip. Yet on tours where the species list is nearer to the low end than to the potential high, I'll add a foray to the POS lagoons so as to quickly add at least a score of species new for the trip.

Among the species commonly seen are brown pelican, purple gallinule, wattled jacana, common black-hawk, yellow-headed caracara, osprey, the boldly marked Trinidad race of the clapper rail, black-bellied and fulvous whistling-ducks, most of the herons

93

including tricolored, little blue and cocoi, collared plover, whimbrel and most migrant species North American shorebirds at some time or other during the year, white-winged and barn swallows, large-billed and yellow-billed terns, black-necked stilt, yellow-chinned spinetail, and all of the more common savannah-inhabiting species.

Birds at the lagoons seem to allow birders to approach them much more closely when the birders are in a vehicle than when they're afoot. For that reason, since at least the beginning of your explorations of the lagoons will be from within a vehicle, be sure to take your camera with you for closeup shots of colorful species and, just as importantly, to enable you to document any rarities you may find.

To reach the POS sewage lagoons, drive west from the intersection of the Churchill-Roosevelt and Uriah Butler Highways. This major intersection is just east of Port-of-Spain (for reference, the mountains you see are to the north). At 4.4km bear right. Don't bear left or you'll exit the highway via the overpass (called a "flyover" in Trinidadian). Just to be sure you don't exit the highway prematurely, stay in the center of the roadway. Pass a few kilometers of mangroves and the Beetham Landfill on your left, over which usually circle thousands of black vultures. At 7.5km watch on the left for a small, low, white building and a sign for NP (National Petroleum). Turn left, entering the lagoon area at the only car-width gap in the chain-link fence. This is the entrance road to the lagoons. Follow it for 0.1km. You'll see a huge white globular tank ahead on the left. The road bends sharply to the left a short distance farther, at the hog farm. Begin birding there.

With a little patience, you should be able to spot or at least hear the unusually colorful Trinidad race of the clapper rail along the ditch on the left. The rail often is in the company of common moorhen and spotted and solitary sandpipers. Watch for common blackhawk, peregrine falcon, and merlin perched atop the numerous dead trees beyond the ditch. Check the mudflats 0.9km farther for thousands of male fiddler crabs waving their enlarged claws to attract females. Fiddler crabs constitute the prey of choice for clapper rails worldwide, and the preference of the Trinidadian race is no exception. This stretch also is good for spotted and solitary sandpipers, collared plover, whimbrel, and yellow-chinned spinetail, whose chatter resembles that of the belted kingfisher.

Just ahead you have a choice of turns. All of these roads follow the perimeters of the four sewage lagoons. All of the lagoons are productive and should be checked for South American strays. The brush on the east side of the lagoon is good for yellow-chinned spinetail. The mangroves along the south side of the lagoons can be good for limpkin, cocoi heron, yellow-crowned night-heron, and bicolored conebill. I've heard the unmistakable calls of wood-rails here as well. Green-throated mango hummingbirds prefer to feed among mangroves, and I've seen them display along this mangrove edge. Scarlet ibis sometimes can be seen from the lagoon area in the evening as they fly in to roost in the Caroni Swamp, which adjoins the lagoon just to the south. Magnificent frigatebirds soar over the Gulf of Paria, which is barely visible to the west.

As you leave the lagoon area, scan the open expanse of earth on the left for resting black skimmers, southern lapwings, sandpipers and plovers, and brown pelican.

HOME CONSTRUCTION LIMITED SEWAGE TREATMENT WORKS (TRINCITY PONDS)
1km, 1 hour

The Home Construction Limited Sewage Treatment Works (hereafter Trincity Ponds) near Trincity is a great place to obtain excellent views of a large number of water-associated species; birding seldom gets easier than this. The works consist of an array of six rectangular impoundments, some covered with large masses of floating water hyacinths. Grassy levees separate the ponds and provide the birder with easy access to all areas.

To reach the Trincity Ponds, travel west along the Churchill-Roosevelt Highway from its intersection with Golden Grove Road, the road that leads from the Churchill-Roosevelt Highway to Piarco International Airport. After about 1.1km, look for a row of Caribbean pines on the left — these trees form the eastern boundary of the facility. At this point make sure you activate your indicator light (turn signal) to warn vehicles behind that you're slowing down. Pull onto the shoulder. At 1.3km take the inconspicuous dirt road on the left, which leads into the Trincity Ponds.

Drive into the area very slowly so as not to alarm nearby birds. As soon as you can see the ponds on the right, stop and scan the water, levees, and sky for wattled jacana; least grebe; large-billed, least, and yellow-billed terns; black skimmer; black-necked stilt; yellow-hooded blackbird; yellow-chinned spinetail; purple gallinule; common moorhen; little and snowy egrets; little blue heron; ringed kingfisher; white-winged swallow; gray-breasted martin; striated and green herons; lesser yellowlegs; ruddy turnstone; various species of sandpipers; laughing gull; least bittern; pied water-tyrant; and white-headed marsh-tyrant. Usually a few spectacled caimans can be found as they bask on the periphery.

This seemingly negligible piece of property currently is the most reliable place in the entire NewWorld at which you can see an accidental species from the Old World, the little egret. From November until March, be sure to examine all white herons you find for one with bluish or grayish (not yellow) facial skin. Look for two long nuchal (head) plumes after January. This will confirm your initial identification.

Drive a little farther, park in the shade of the Caribbean pines if possible, and walk along the dikes, scanning the water and hyacinths, the banks, and the sky. Be attentive, as it's easy to overlook some of the more secretive species, especially those lurking among the hyacinths. With luck you may even spot a masked duck hiding among them.

CHAGUARAMAS AREA
10km, half day

Located northwest of Port-of-Spain near the end of the prong that extends toward the Boca Islands and the Paria Peninsula of Venezuela, the Chaguaramas area until recently has been relatively inaccessible to birders because of its military status. Recently the Chaguaramas Development Authority has granted birders limited access to certain parts of the area, which is bird-rich because of its long period of dormancy. Some areas are covered with tall grasses that support populations of such hard-to-find species as sooty grassquit.

The staff of the National Park Department has compiled a checklist of the birds of Chaguaramas, which they hope to update through the assistance of visiting birders.

You'll need permission to enter the Chaguaramas area. Tour guides must pay a fee of TT$100 to the Chaguaramas Development Authority for a license to conduct birding tours. Tour leaders must limit the group size to 20 persons. Other persons who wish to bird in the Chaguaramas area must first obtain a permit (TT$5.00) from the Chaguaramas National Park Department of the Chaguaramas Development Authority:

Address —   Chaguaramas Development Authority
              P.O. Box 3162
              Chaguaramas, Trinidad, W.I.
              (809) 625-1503/634-4364/4349 voice
              (809) 625-2465 fax

You must check with the Chaguaramas Development Authority Security, located at the Police Post, before proceeding into the area. In addition to the birding permit, you must obtain separate permission to visit Tetron, Staubles Bay, Omega Tracking Station, and the Rifle Range, all of which are restricted areas. You can make all arrangements by telephone and pay for the permits on the first day of your birdwatching in the area if you wish.

To reach the Chaguaramas area, follow the Western Main Road west from Port-of-Spain, bearing left at every reasonable opportunity. When you reach the marina called Power Boats on your left, stop to scan the power lines and boat masts for American kestrel. This is the only place I know in all of Trinidad to find this species, which ironically is not uncommon in nearby Venezuela.

The sight of a guard station in the middle of the road will confirm that you've reached the entrance to the Chaguaramas restricted area. Stop here and obtain your permits and all other materials you may need. Once past the guard station, you can bird at your discretion. Most of the roads that lead north toward the heights of Mount Catharine are worth birding. The coastal scrub at the western tip of the peninsula has the greatest potential in Trinidad for hosting Venezuelan strays such as streaked saltator and scrub flycatcher.

After birding the Chaguaramas area, you may wish to visit the Tucker Valley, another promising area in western Trinidad. This pleasant gap between mountains lies about two-thirds of the way between Port-of-Spain and Chaguaramas. Upon exiting the Chaguaramas area, take the first major left (Tucker Valley Road) at a V intersection. Tucker Valley Road leads through areas that to me resemble the high parks (intermountain valleys) of Colorado. You'll find many places to pull off the road and bird.

If you continue all the way to the end of Tucker Valley Road, you'll come to the remains of a World War II dance hall at Corozal Point, overlooking Maqueripe Bay. Several rugged trails lead west, up and into the scrub, where you can seek stray Venezuelan species.

To return to Port-of-Spain, retrace your route through the Tucker Valley, then turn left onto the Western Main Road.

BIRDING ON TOBAGO

Birding on Tobago is considerably different from birding in
Trinidad. Tobago is small enough so that you can investigate much
of it during a short visit. As land owners continue to abandon cultivated areas, extensive tracts of former plantations are reverting to a
wild state, providing new habitat for wildlife. Thus the future of
the birds of Tobago appears to be promising, except for that of
species such as boobies, which are still hunted despite protection
under law. Another happy thought — there are *no* poisonous
snakes on Tobago! And no chiggers, either, so you can forge
through waist-high grass with abandon.

About 90% of the human population of Tobago lives in the southern third of the island. North of the capital city of Scarborough, the
land becomes mountainous and rugged, more so in general than in
Trinidad. Extremes can be found in climate and habitat on this
mite of an island, with lush rainforests along the central spine and
xeric-scrub deserts on the windward sides of islets such as St. Giles
and Little Tobago. Although fewer species of land birds live on
Tobago than in Trinidad, and fewer individuals of each species,
that aspect is offset by their extreme tameness.

Incidentally, imitations of ferruginous pygmy-owl work poorly on
Tobago because the owl isn't resident. Local guides such as
Adolphus James can imitate the calls of nearly all songbirds on
Tobago and attract them into view in that manner.

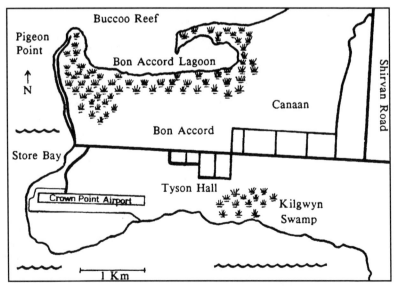

*Southern Tobago showing Crown Point Airport area, Pigeon Point, Bon Accord Lagoon,
and Kilgwyn Swamp.*

If you have only a brief time to stay in Tobago, plan to visit at least these four sites — the mangrove swamps in the south, the central highlands, Hillsborough Dam, and Little Tobago Island. By so doing you'll afford yourself the best opportunities to observe those species found in Tobago but not in Trinidad: red-billed tropicbird, rufous-vented chachalaca, striped owl, white-tailed sabrewing, red-crowned woodpecker, olivaceous woodcreeper, white-fringed antwren, blue-backed manakin, Venezuelan flycatcher, Caribbean martin, scrub greenlet, black-faced grassquit, and variable seedeater.

CROWN POINT AIRPORT AREA
5km, 3 hours

Whereas most airports are avian deserts, devoid of all but the most pernicious species of birds, Crown Point Airport in Tobago actually provides rewarding birding action. For example, on a visit in mid-June I tallied the following species in less than an hour while within sight of the runway: brown booby; brown pelican; magnificent frigatebird; cattle egret; yellow-crowned night-heron; laughing gull; royal, sandwich, roseate, common, bridled, and sooty terns; brown noddy; eared and white-tipped doves; ruddy ground-dove; smooth-billed ani; ruby-topaz hummingbird; red-crowned woodpecker; yellow-bellied elaenia; brown-crested flycatcher; tropical and gray kingbirds; Caribbean martin; bare-eyed thrush; tropical mockingbird; scrub greenlet; bananaquit; blue-gray tanager; black-faced grassquit; carib grackle; and crested oropendola.

Begin your explorations from the airport main exit, making the first possible left turn, just beyond a chain-link fence, onto Milford Road. Follow whatever roads are currently open, heading toward the end of the runway. Milford Road, for example, follows the perimeter of the airport. Bird first along the beach and then through an open savannah to sea cliffs on the south side of the island. Park along the beach at every access point and scan the surf for brown booby, brown pelican, laughing gull, and the tern species named above. Watch overhead for magnificent frigatebirds and extremely low-flying jets thundering past on their final approach to Crown Point Airport.

Follow Milford Road around the airport grounds for 2.5km, scanning the chain-link fence for grassquits and for ruddy-breasted seedeater, which becomes more common when the airport allows the grass to grow high. At the end of Milford Road, walk along the conspicuous trails that lead to the sea cliffs. From there you can scan the channel ("Galleons Passage") between Trinidad and Tobago for the species named above as they scale over the waves or rest on the rocks just offshore and below you. Wherever possible, push through the thornless beach plum trees around the cattle fields to the cliffs. The cattle are armed with formidable horns but are nevertheless docile and even shy. Avoid those with calves.

Work your way east along the shoreline as far as you wish, watching for common barn-owl and white-tailed nightjar roosting in the dense woods. If you continue to follow the shoreline, you'll come to Kilgwyn Swamp, a privately owned wetland that hosts a population of about 30 white-cheeked pintails. An easier access to Kilgwyn Swamp is from the eastern end, which you can easily find by driving east instead of west as you leave the airport, then taking all the turns that head toward the eastern end of the runway.

If you have time, explore the caves in the sea cliffs below; despite evidence to the contrary, legend has it that this stretch of beach is the site of Robinson Crusoe's cave.

PIGEON POINT
10km, half day

As I'm writing this, the Bon Accord Lagoon area, like so many other great birding spots, is under development into a housing project, so this section soon may be obsolete.

A northward-pointing peninsula northeast of Crown Point Airport consists of stunningly beautiful white beaches set off against a background of coconut palms. Pigeon Point is in every way a paradise for the photographer. Just landward, cabanas give way to a mangrove swamp that rings Bon Accord Lagoon. The wetlands that encircle Bon Accord Lagoon provide a rather rare habitat on Tobago. Bird species that you can find here include pied-billed grebe, osprey, rufous-vented chachalaca, black-bellied and lesser golden-plovers, migrant North American sandpipers, eared and white-tipped doves, white-tailed nightjar, copper-rumped hummingbird, ruby-topaz hummingbird, barred antshrike, white-fringed antwren, brown-crested flycatcher, gray kingbird, Caribbean martin, bare-eyed thrush, scrub greenlet, migrant North American warblers, black-faced grassquit, and surprisingly musical shiny cowbirds.

To reach Pigeon Point, turn right at the airport main exit onto Milford Road, passing a red-and-white radio tower on the left. At 1.0km follow the arrow on the blue-and-white sign to Pigeon Point. Drive straight ahead toward the Caribbean. This slight indentation in the western coast is called Store Bay. Follow the road around a curve to the right. At 2.1km turn right at the sign "Fisherman's Row" and park.

Search the edges of the mangrove-lined lake ahead of you for common moorhen and yellow-crowned night-heron. Continue in your car through the entrance gate, paying your TT$5-per-person fee. Proceed along Coconut Drive, passing a checkpoint at 2.9km where a guard will tear the corner off your entrance ticket. Continue past the beachside cabanas, following the road to the right. The bright blue-green bay in front of you at this point is Nylon Pool, famous for its sandy, stoneless bottom. Its name comes from the resemblance of the color of its water to that of prototypic nylon.

Bear right at the Y intersection at 3.4km. The road degenerates here and becomes rutted and primitive but still driveable. At 3.6km turn right at an obscure Y; a left turn here will put you on the beach instead of in mangroves. If the lane is muddy, park when you reach 3.9km and walk the lane ahead of you into the coconut/mangrove swamp; otherwise, drive on a bit farther and park there. The lane winds through an open mangrove woodland for the next 0.5km. Red mangroves dominate the swamp, with white mangroves on the southern edge. Abundant here are brown-crested flycatcher, gray kingbird, yellow-crowned night-heron, copper-rumped hummingbird, ruby-topaz hummingbird, barred antshrike, and shiny cowbird. When birding alone I've found that pishing brings in all of those species to arm's length or less, especially if I've remained absolutely still and dispersed the pishing sound between my fingers.

From time to time as you bird this wetland, try pishing and whistling the call of the ferruginous pygmy-owl to attract any migrants from Trinidad or South America that may be on the island. For added fun, try whistling the call of the eastern screech-owl after the responding songbirds have become jaded to your other imitations. Sometimes neotropical migrants such as American redstart, northern waterthrush, and prothonotary warbler flash into view in response to the call of the eastern screech-owl.

Throughout the swamp, common moorhens and rufous-vented chachalacas create a ruckus in the mangroves, though they keep out of sight. Where the lane enters a wide, grassy pasture, cross a conspicuous ditch on the right and try to remain inconspicuous yourself as you walk to the tip of the short peninsula that overlooks a tidal lake. Use the mangroves to cloak your approach. Look for tricolored, little blue, and genuine green herons (not striated as in Trinidad), whimbrel, black-bellied and lesser golden-plover, and white-cheeked pintail. Some of the whimbrel belong to the European race *phaeopus*, with white rump and underwings. Search carefully on the mangrove roots for sleeping white-tailed nightjars. Large iguanas sometimes can be seen gleaning foliage in the crowns of the mangroves; when disturbed, they hurl themselves into the water below with a resounding splash.

Back on the lane, you'll shortly come to a concrete footbridge. Turn right, and as you proceed look along the wet channels for shorebirds and waders. Explore all passable dikes around this wet area, noting the birds flying over, which include the ever-present magnificent frigatebirds and cattle egrets.

If you continue on, bearing left wherever possible, you can stay in the swamp as it turns north then west on the Golden Grove peninsula. Eventually you'll reach the shore of the lagoon and can enjoy a sunny beachside stroll back to your car, complete with a case of sunstroke if you've forgotten your hat.

BUCCOO MARSH
10km, 2 hours

As I mentioned earlier, wetlands are scarce on Tobago. Migrant shorebirds thus have few choices of where to feed and loaf. Since Tobago seems to be a magnet for Old World strays, especially shorebirds and large waders, I'd recommend that you try to visit all the wetlands you can when you bird Tobago.

Adolphus James first showed me Buccoo Marsh in the early 1980s. It's actually a swamp, not a marsh; I was taught that "a swamp has trees and water to the knees, a marsh has grass and water to the ... knees as well." Marsh or swamp, the area's been one of my favorite Tobago birding sites ever since.

(By the way, years later I was able to return the favor by showing Adolphus his first Wilson's phalarope, at Buccoo Marsh. It was the first record for Tobago as well. I added Adolphus as a coauthor of the published record, so now he's immortal.)

Among the bird species you can find in the Buccoo Marsh area are pied-billed grebe, least grebe, masked duck, anhinga, osprey, merlin, rufous-vented chachalaca, black-bellied and lesser golden-plovers, black-bellied and fulvous whistling-ducks, scarlet ibis on rare occasions, a wide range of resident and migrant herons and sandpipers including more Eurasian strays than stands to reason, eared and white-tipped doves, white-tailed nightjar, copper-rumped hummingbird, ruby-topaz hummingbird, barred antshrike, white-fringed antwren, brown-crested flycatcher, gray kingbird, Caribbean martin, bare-eyed thrush, scrub greenlet, a few migrant North American warblers including prothonotary, black-faced grassquit, and shiny cowbirds.

If you have the opportunity, visit Buccoo Marsh early in the morning, when the birds are most active and the sun is behind you. Late afternoon visits require you to look almost directly into the sun, when the sizzling blaze renders colors more black-and-white than saturated.

To reach Buccoo Marsh, turn right at the airport main exit onto Milford Road, passing a red-and-white radio tower on the left. Continue on for about 2.0km as the road gradually bears eastward. You'll pass through a heavily populated stretch of road before coming to Shirvan Road on your left. Turn left onto Shirvan Road and proceed for just over 2.0km. Not far after you pass the intersection with Buccoo Road on the right and then Golden Grove Road on the left, the road curves to the left. As it begins to straighten out and then to curve to the right a bit, watch for a gated wire fence on your left. That fence encloses a grazed cattle field and is all that separates you from Buccoo Marsh.

Park on the left, well off the road. If you encounter the picturesque groundskeeper during your visit, pay him the TT$1 per person entrance fee (or more if the fee has increased). If you find no one about, you might consider sending your fee to Adolphus James with a polite request that he forward the money to the landed gentry at his convenience.

I leave it to you to get yourself to the other side of the fence — over, under, around, or through. To prevent the cattle from exiting onto the roadway, if you unlatch the gate to allow for a dignified passage, you must reaffix it as it was when you arrived.

Once inside the fence, proceed a short distance, then stop and search the guava trees on both sides of the path for brown-crested flycatcher, scrub greenlet, white-fringed antwren, and barred antshrike. Red-crowned woodpeckers often are noisy and conspicuous on the hole-ridden coconut palms throughout the area. Watch for cowpies as you transit the field.

Almost any of the paths heading away from the road will take you to the marsh, but the best initial views are from somewhat to the left of the main cowpath. Be careful of the thorny shrubs as you silently make your way through the open brush for a few hundred meters until you can see the semicircular, grass-bordered, mangrove-backed lagoon ahead of you. If you have a telescope, set it up here and scan first the water's edge, then the hyacinth-graced lagoon, and finally the foliage on the other side of the open water.

Along the marshy edge look for shorebirds including both species of yellowlegs, wattled jacana, and southern lapwing and for long-legged waders including little egret, tricolored heron, and green heron. Besides yellowlegs, the most common small shorebirds are western, semipalmated, solitary, pectoral, and spotted sandpipers. When few birds are present, those you find will often include a rarity for some reason. For example, you can imagine my great pleasure at creeping up on the lagoon to find the Wilson's phalarope feeding at the feet of a little egret. Few other species were present, but I was more than satisfied.

In the emergent vegetation, especially along the shore on the right, look for whimbrel (including the Eurasian race *phaeopus* with white rump and underwings), common moorhen, both species of coot, both species of night-heron, masked duck, and any rails or crakes that may be present.

In the open water scan for whistling-ducks, white-cheeked pintail, and migrant North American ducks such as blue-winged teal. The mangroves that grow above the open water usually contribute at least one anhinga, often with outstretched wings.

When you're finished with your initial survey, spend a few minutes exploring the edges of the lagoon to your right and beyond, although you can't penetrate very far into the mangroves because of high water. In the mangroves you may find gray kingbird along with a few shorebirds resting on the mangrove roots.

Retrace your path to the opposite side of the lagoon. Working very slowly, wend your way around the perimeter of the lagoon, following it as it continues left. Northern waterthrush and prothonotary warbler sometimes are found in this intimate little site. Beyond, in the small mangrove islands, are nesting cattle egrets with the sporadic visitor such as snowy or little egret. As you break out of cover, scan the wet grass ahead and to your left for whimbrel and other shorebirds.

Most birding tour guides turn back at this point because the ground gets mucky and the woods thick, but if you have time you may wish to continue birding beyond the grassy area. Eventually you'll be in a mangrove swamp that's contiguous with that of Pigeon Point.

To return to your car, you can either retrace your lagoon-side route or make a line-of-sight plunge through the thorny vegetation. Just remember that if your clothes are ripped to shreds in the process, the modest Tobagonians may think less of you.

Reservoir behind Hillsborough Dam, reliable for least grebe and Caribbean martin.

HILLSBOROUGH DAM AND OLD CASTARA ROAD
64km, 1 day

Before visiting this site, you should obtain a WASA permit. See the section on the Arena Forest for instructions on how to obtain one.

Rainforests in Tobago are restricted to the higher elevations. This tour will take you into the mountains of the Main Ridge, first to the Hillsborough Dam, a freshwater reservoir, then deeper into the forest along an ancient rustic trail. On this trip you should see least grebe, blue-crowned motmot, rufous-tailed jacamar, blue-backed manakin, and about forty other species of birds.

From Crown Point Airport turn right and drive to Scarborough via the satellite-photo-visible four-lane Claude Noel Highway, following the signs toward Scarborough.

("What's this wonderful divided highway doing on a tiny island where, if all the cars were parked end-to-end, they still couldn't begin to make it look like rush-hour?" you may ask. The answer is that when Tobago asked Trinidad for money to extend Crown Point Airport's runway so as to accommodate international flights, Trinidad gave them this highway instead. Claude Noel was a world-famous boxer from Tobago.)

At 10.4km, turn left and drive 0.3km to the summit of the hill for a fine scenic view of the capital city of Scarborough, which hugs Rockly Bay. Return to the Claude Noel Highway, turn left, and

105

continue past Scarborough for several kilometers beyond the point at which the expressway turns into a two-lane blacktopped road. Just as you enter the village of Mount St. George, you'll cross a bridge, with the Atlantic Ocean just to the right. Watch carefully on the left for a large wooden store followed immediately by a white house at a Y intersection. Turn left onto this steep paved road (unmarked; Mount St. George-Castara Road) that leads to Hillsborough Dam. Another landmark to watch for, as you start to climb the hill, is a sign on the right that says "Notice, Tobago House of Assembly." If you miss this turn, take the next left; that road intersects the Mount St. George-Castara Road a few kilometers farther on.

The pavement ends once you leave the town of Mount St. George. The actual mount of Mount St. George is on the left as you climb this steep road. Pass a quarry and stay to the right at the Y intersection. Watch for blue-crowned motmots, rufous-tailed jacamars, and orange-winged parrots flying across the road and for short-tailed and gray-rumped swifts plummeting along the cliff faces. After much twisting and turning, often through fabulous scenery with splendid vistas of the seacoast, the road brings you to a group of beige-and-blue buildings, which is the water control station for Hillsborough Dam. Park here and check the powerlines along the road for Caribbean martin and gray kingbirds, the *Croton* bushes for nesting black-throated mango, and the reservoir for least grebe, anhinga, neotropic cormorant, and gray-rumped swift. At the dam itself watch for migrant swallows, including barn and bank swallows. Watch for spectacled caimans basking along the margin of the reservoir.

Continue along the increasingly obscure road and drive up the hill beyond the dam. Stop wherever paths lead into the woods. Explore the grassy fringes for seedeaters and grassquits, the forest edges for collared trogon, golden-olive and red-rumped woodpeckers, stripe-breasted spinetail, yellow-bellied elaenia, fuscous flycatcher, and white-winged becard, and the deeper rainforest for olivaceous woodcreeper, gray-throated leaftosser, white-fringed antwren, and blue-backed manakin.

At the next intersection turn right onto Old Castara Road, park, and bird as far as you wish on foot. This road is one of the best high elevation sites for birding in Tobago. Pishing often attracts flocks of up to a dozen different species.

When you've finished birding, retrace your route back to Scarborough.

LITTLE TOBAGO ("BIRD OF PARADISE") ISLAND
95km, 1 day

Obtain prior permission to visit Little Tobago Island from the Forestry section of the Department of Agriculture, Forestry and Fisheries of the Tobago House of Assembly. You can obtain information from the Botanic Station, Scarborough (809-639-3265) or from the Forestry Office, Windward Road, Mount St. George, Tobago.

About 2km off the northeastern coast of Tobago lies Little Tobago Island, one of Trinidad and Tobago's most impressive wildlife sanctuaries. The island comprises only 113 ha (280 acres), much of it very hilly and steep, and attains a maximum elevation of 140m. Fan palms and gumbo limbo trees predominate in the forest. The cliff-sided eastern (windward) side is dominated by cactus and other xeric shrubs. The island's main attraction for birders lies in its essentially pelagic situation. Nowhere else on either Trinidad or Tobago can you obtain such comfortable and close views of nesting red-billed tropicbirds, brown boobies, laughing gulls, and bridled and sooty terns. Magnificent frigatebirds and red-footed boobies nest on nearby St. Giles island and can be seen in the distance from the overlooks on the northeastern side of Little Tobago Island.

The island derives its name from the introduced greater bird-of-paradise. This species, formerly the focal point of birding on Little Tobago Island, was practically wiped out by Hurricane Flora in 1963. Numbers dwindled quickly thereafter. The species wasn't recorded after the early 1980s and is undoubtedly extirpated from Little Tobago Island. Rumor has it that the last individual of this colonial species was observed attempting to blend in with a colony of crested oropendolas, which would have nothing to do with the much larger species. On a more positive note, more than 50 species of other birds occur regularly on Little Tobago Island.

Please be aware that your own canteen may hold the only supply of drinking water available on the island and that some trails require strenuous hiking.

The trip from southern Tobago to Little Tobago Island and back is an all-day affair. To afford you more time on the island, I'd recommend that you spend the previous night at the north end of the island, at either the Blue Waters Inn or at Turpin's Cottages. Birds are most active just after dawn, and the sea at that time is usually fairly calm, so if you're traveling from the Crown Point area you should leave your hotel well before first light so as to reach Little Tobago Island before the midday lull.

To reach Little Tobago Island from southern Tobago, follow the Claude Noel Highway north past Scarborough. Continue for about 40km, staying on the main road, which rivals Blanchisseuse Road in Trinidad in the numbers of its twists and turns.

As you enter the town of Roxborough, you'll note a fire station on your right. At this point you have an opportunity to get in some rainforest birding if you wish. The Roxborough-Bloody Bay Road is the easiest and safest road upon which to reach Tobago's Main Ridge with its pristine rainforest. If you chose to takethis side excursion, turn left at this point ontothe Roxborough-Bloody Bay Road. This scenic, well paved drive transects the Main Ridge and affords endless opportunities to bird in the moist, cool heights. Almost any trail that leads off the road will be productive. You may wish to try the Branch 2 Trace and theRoxborough Valley Trace, although most tour groups proceed directly to the summit and bird the well-marked Gilpin Trace.

Target birds in the Tobago rainforest are white-tailed sabrewing hummingbird, blue-backed manakin, yellow-legged thrush, stripe-breasted spinetail, Venezuelan flycatcher, and great black-hawk.

If you decide to forego birding the rainforest, or after you've been there, continue through the town of Roxborough and about 12km farther drop down, almost literally, into tiny Speyside.

You have several choices for arranging the 2-km trip across Tyrrell's Bay to Little Tobago Island. The manager at the Blue Water's Inn may arrange in advance to have a boat ready to take you there, or you may opt to negotiate for the trip with the fishermen in Speyside when you arrive. In any case, if you arrange with a boatman to be dropped off and then picked up later, be sure to confirm the time at which he'll return. If you chose the latter arrangement, take extra provisions with you in case rough seas prevent the boatman from picking you up as scheduled.

Rates for the round trip vary considerably depending mostly upon the number of persons traveling together. At this time a typical fare is about US$10. The fare increases if you want the boatman to wait there for you. Be sure to wrap your binoculars, camera, and other optical equipment in waterproof material, preferably within nested plastic zip-lock bags, to protect them from the salt spray. While crossing, watch for hawksbill, leatherback, and other species of sea turtles that nest along the coasts of Trinidad and Tobago from late February to late August and for large barracudas (don't trail your hands in the water).

The brief crossing occasionally is rough, especially during the change of tides, but exploring Little Tobago Island and viewing the colonies of seabirds is worth the slight discomfort. I'm a classic case of a person who's susceptible to *mal de mer*. I've found that standing up in the boat, where possible, helps me stay seasick-free. If the boat has a glass bottom, I can count on getting nauseated just by viewing the rolling, pitching, yawing undersea life through the glass. If you have any tendency at all toward seasickness, try to stand during the trip so long as you have something secure onto which to hold, get the most wind in your face that you can, don't try to use your binoculars until you have both feet on solid ground, and avoid looking through the glass bottom of the boat. The good news is that the boat trip is short, the sea is usually fairly calm, the boatman is interested in keeping his boat out of major swells, and once ashore any slight disorientation you may pick up on the trip across will dissipate instantly.

Both the departure and landing are wet, meaning that you need to wade to and from the boat. The waves may wash as high as your thighs, so carry your belongings, including your dry shoes and socks, high over your head. The boatman knows his turf; listen carefully to his instructions about when to get on and off, and when he says to go, GO!

Once ashore, stop at the beachside hut to dry your feet and put on your shoes. Don't be alarmed by the loud rustling and scratching around you in the forest; the source usually is one of the hundreds of feral chickens on the island. A set of concrete steps leads up the hill to the warden's station. The burrows in the soft earth in the banks along the way are dug by Audubon's shearwaters, which nest in January and February, arriving and departing from their nests at night. Cautious use of a flashlight may provide you with a view of a shearwater in its tunnel.

Continue up the hill to the warden's house. Check the Visitors' Log to see if anyone else is on the island with you. If an official is present, show evidence of the permission you obtained to visit the island. On the other hand, if the house is vacant, as it almost always is, leave the names and addresses of the members in your party, the date, and how long you plan to remain on the island. Before departing from the island, it also would be courteous to leave a copy of your sightings list at the warden's house, or send them to me upon your return and I'll make sure they reach the proper people.

From the warden's house continue east, watching for white-tailed nightjars (conspicuous at dawn and dusk only), until you reach the cactus-covered cliff on the east side of the island. Stop at the shelter. Just ahead of you, on the cliffs to the left, are the nesting colonies of red-billed tropicbird, brown booby, sooty tern, brown noddy, and laughing gull. If you're quiet and move slowly, you may be able to photograph these species at close range. December through February marks the peak nesting period for red-billed tropicbird. Brown boobies nest mostly in July and again in January and February. Sooty terns nest during February and March, brown noddies in March, and laughing gulls in May.

Observing red-footed boobies usually requires you to train your binoculars or telescope on the long, thin island that lies about halfway to the horizon. The water just beyond that island is the main thoroughfare for red-footed boobies traveling to and from deep offshore waters to their nests and roosts on St. Giles Island, the distant island to your left. Watch carefully for any boobies with white rumps; those are your quarries.

Return to and pass the warden's house. Take a left on the conspicuous trail that leads south along a ridge. Here you may see such species as broad-winged hawk (March through May), white-tipped dove, pale-vented pigeon, chivi vireo, and crested oropendola. Watch for roseate terns feeding offshore. Bridled and sooty terns also are common just off the island. Blue-crowned motmots are easy to find, and Venezuelan flycatchers are particularly abundant but sedentary. Seedeaters are rare throughout Trinidad and Tobago, but Lesson's and yellow-bellied seedeaters are reportedly possible to find on Little Tobago from May until October.

Rufous-tailed jacamar, by Michelle Altman

TARGET SPECIES IN TRINIDAD AND TOBAGO

The following list includes species of unusual status or patchy distribution and those frequently missed by visitors. It excludes widespread species and most accidentals while emphasizing the birding locales described previously in this book. As far as possible, bird names and their arrangement follow the *A.O.U. Check-list of North American Birds*, Sixth Edition, 1983 (American Ornithologists' Union, Allen Press, Lawrence, Kansas, USA. xxix + 887 pp.).

Little tinamou A pigeon-sized, upright, strictly terrestrial species that prefers open second-growth forests with a high, dense canopy; Mount St. Benedict, Arena Forest, Brigand Hill. Responds to taped recordings of its call but not to vocal imitations. Calls throughout the day.

Least grebe Breed at Trincity Ponds and Port-of-Spain Sewage Lagoons (especially in the southwestern pond). Also reported from Caroni Swamp, Pointe-à-Pierre Wild Fowl Trust, Hollis Reservoir, and on Tobago at Hillsborough Dam and Buccoo Marsh. Apparently more common now than formerly. V-shaped wake is more conspicuous than the tiny bird itself.

Shearwaters and petrels Almost never seen from shore in Trinidad anywhere but at Manzanilla Beach on the east coast, but possible to see from shore on Tobago. Also possible to observe at rare intervals from the Trinidad-Tobago ferry.

Great shearwater Seen several times in recent years in small numbers from oil drilling platform 24km east of Galeota Point, June 14-17; should be looked for off Manzanilla Beach during that period.

Audubon's shearwater Breeds on Little Tobago Island. Comes and goes from its burrow only at night and thus is difficult to observe. In Trinidad and Tobago I've never seen this species away from its burrow.

Leach's storm-petrel Rarely seen offshore, February through early June, along Manzanilla Beach, where occasionally found sick or dead as well. Most promising spot from which to scan is the first pullout on the left after the road descends to the beach from Lower Manzanilla, just after the bridge. Persistent scanning usually pays off.

Red-billed tropicbird Specialty of Little Tobago Island, breeding on cliffs on ocean side; hard to find anywhere else but off northern Tobago. Seen a few times from the Trinidad-Tobago ferry.

Brown booby Very rarely seen from mainland Trinidad but common offshore on Tobago, especially in north. Seen at rare intervals from Trinidad-Tobago ferry.

Red-footed booby Very rarely seen in Trinidad and uncommon offshore on Tobago; breeds on St. Giles Island. Hard to find anywhere but far off to the north of Little Tobago Island; look for the white diamond formed by the feathers of the rump and lower back. Brown booby has dark rump.

Brown pelican Distribution expanding; undergoing a population explosion in Trinidad.

Neotropic cormorant Formerly called olivaceous cormorant. Pointe-à-Pierre Wild Fowl Trust (1000+), singles often seen in Caroni Swamp and Arena Dam area. Apparently prefers saltwater for fishing, freshwater for roosting. Previously a nonbreeding visitor, now a resident breeder at Pointe-à-Pierre Wild Fowl Trust.

Anhinga Arena Dam, Hillsborough Dam, Pointe-à-Pierre Wild Fowl Trust, Nariva Swamp; Buccoo Marsh, Tobago. Prefers freshwater lakes with dense, overhanging foliage.

Gray heron Recorded only in 1959 but easily confused with great blue heron. *White, not rufous, thighs* confirm identification of this Eurasian species.

Pinnated bittern Nariva and Caroni Swamps; uncommon, inconspicuous, prone to remain motionless with bill pointed skyward at about a 70° angle. Most easily seen 3-4 p.m.

Stripe-backed bittern Caroni Swamp and El Socorro Marsh; uncommon, inconspicuous, increasingly rare. Most visible 3-4 p.m. Straw-colored back with conspicuous dark streaks and lack of contrast between back and wings help separate it from least bittern. Ratio of sightings of stripe-backed to least is about 5-to-1.

Least bittern Increasingly rare; Nariva and Caroni Swamps. Caroni resident population about 20 individuals. Most easily seen 3-4 p.m.

Rufescent tiger-heron Rare, hard to find; the only recent reports are from Nariva and south Trinidad. Try Nariva or Caroni Swamps at twilight, especially marshes at Caroni near tour boat docks. Prefers lowland marshes and swamp/mangrove forest; hides in tall grasses and sedges like a bittern.

Cocoi heron Arena Dam, Pointe-à-Pierre Wild Fowl Trust, Nariva and Caroni Swamps; watch for it to fly across open channels.

Prefers coastal sides of salt- and freshwater swamps and lake edges; solitary.

Little egret/western reef-heron Trincity Ponds, Port-of-Spain Sewage Lagoons; occasionally in the few wetlands on Tobago, especially Buccoo Marsh. Increasing in numbers in southeastern Caribbean, with more than 50 records for the New World; many records from Trinidad and Tobago. First South American record (dark phase "western reef-heron") was in Nariva Swamp in January 1986; up to 5 were on Tobago in June 1986. "Reef-heron" is like little blue heron with white chin, black legs, yellow feet. Little egret (white phase) like snowy egret but with 2 long plumes (seasonal), bluish or gray lores, duller yellow feet.

Reddish egret Unknown to local guides but seen twice in recent years, mid-January and October.

Green heron Trincity Ponds, Caroni Swamp; Buccoo Marsh, Tobago. Striated heron for several years was lumped by taxonomists with green heron. Recent proof that the two species don't interbreed has forced ornithologists to resurrect striated heron as a full species. The two species are easily distinguished. Striated heron is light gray on face, neck, and breast, in contrast to corresponding reddish-brown areas on green heron. Striated is overall much lighter in color than green heron and has well defined black cap. Both species occupy same wetland habitat, but striated heron has never been detected on Tobago.

Striated heron See preceding species.

Boat-billed heron Common (2500+ in Caroni Swamp) but roost is inaccessible and species is nocturnal; difficult to spot during daylight hours because of secretive nature and impenetrable habitat (mangroves). Can be seen as fly-bys by use of spotlight at night about 0.5km west of Caroni Swamp boat tour docks; seek permission from Wildlife Section, Forestry Division.

Scarlet ibis Guaranteed on Caroni Swamp boat trips at dusk as they fly to roost from feeding grounds at South Oropuche wetlands and Venezuela; also possible as fly-overs at El Socorro Marsh and Port-of-Spain Sewage Lagoons. Numbers fluctuate from year to year, currently high.

Glossy ibis Recent population expansion, now regular (usually single birds) near San Fernando, Caroni Swamp (southern), and along the southwest coast. As with lesser yellow-headed vulture, any day now some keen birder will carefully scrutinize a presumptive glossy ibis and discover that it's actually a green ibis.

Roseate spoonbill Rare; Pointe-à-Pierre Wild Fowl Trust, Caroni Swamp; flocks of 10 or more possible on Caroni Swamp boat trips but irregular. Very conspicuous and hard to miss if present. Roost in trees and feed on mudflats or in shallow water.

Horned screamer Extirpated; last recorded from Nariva Swamp.

Fulvous whistling-duck Port-of-Spain Sewage Lagoons. Increasing in Trinidad as a result of release programs; still rare. Prefers marshland with open pools and high grasses or lakes with grassy edges and islands; also found near rice fields in mixed flocks with black-bellied whistling-duck.

White-faced whistling-duck Extirpated through overhunting; breeding stock at Pointe-à-Pierre Wild Fowl Trust may account for recent sightings at El Socorro Marsh.

Black-bellied whistling-duck Caroni and Nariva Swamps; Buccoo Marsh, Tobago. Pointe-à-Pierre release program reestablished breeding population. Frequents open water, marshes with open pools, large bodies of water with grassy edges and islands; also rice fields.

Muscovy duck Occasionally reported Nariva and southernmost swamps (Icacos); widespread domestication precludes determination of origin of such individuals.

White-cheeked pintail Rare; Tobago (Pigeon Point, Kilgwyn Swamp, Buccoo Marsh) and Point Lisas, Trinidad. Fully protected but very wary. Breeds at Pointe-à-Pierre Wild Fowl Trust.

Masked duck Uncommon; El Socorro Marsh, Trincity Ponds; Buccoo Marsh, Tobago. Rarely seen; sits very low in the water and submerges rather than taking flight. Prefers areas with dense growth of water hyacinth and other herbaceous plants.

Lesser yellow-headed vulture Nariva; possible recent sighting of a lone bird, identification based on yellow head and low, level flight. Most (all?) other reports have been misidentifications of resident yellow-naped (Venezuelan) race of turkey vulture. Lesser yellow-headed vulture has white upper primaries but is otherwise extremely similar in appearance to a turkey vulture. Unlike turkey vulture, very partial to marshes and wet savannas.

King vulture Rare; Northern Range. Recent records of adults and immatures near Blanchisseuse, Heights of Aripo, village of Brasso Seco in central Northern Range.

114 **Gray-headed kite** Increasing, common but local; most often seen in Northern Range, especially lower Arima Valley.

Hook-billed kite Rare in wet savannahs and swamps; possibly overlooked because of sedentary nature. Recent record of three individuals at Wallerfield.

Pearl kite Uncommon, partial to coconut palms and telephone lines; most sightings along Mayaro Road, Pointe-à-Pierre, and Chaguanas; has bred at Pointe-à-Pierre. Also regular at Wallerfield and along Churchill-Roosevelt Highway east of Orange Grove Road. Behavior similar to that of American kestrel.

White-tailed kite Formerly rare but increasing in Nariva (and possibly Caroni) Swamps; characteristic hovering is distinctive at a great distance.

Double-toothed kite Uncommon but frequent in Arima Valley; small, fast-flying hawk whose flight strongly resembles that of sharp-shinned hawk.

Long-winged harrier Uncommon; rice fields across highway from Caroni boat docks, southern end of Caroni Swamp (Caroni Sluice area), and Oropuche Lagoon. Probably overlooked because of similarity to low-flying turkey vulture. Behavior similar to that of northern harrier — flies with bounding low flight, hovers, then drops on prey. Persistent scanning usually turns up at least one individual, along with peregrine falcon and merlin (Nov.-Mar.).

White hawk Possibly world's most beautiful raptor. With patience possible to spot from most overlooks in Northern Range; less common to the south. Often puzzles birders because *not all-white*; wings, most of tail black.

Rufous crab-hawk Rare; a few records from Nariva Swamp and one from Pointe-à-Pierre. Similar in appearance to immature savanna hawk. Sedentary.

Common black-hawk Widespread and abundant, particularly in Northern Range. Often confused with next species. As ffrench aptly points out, in flight best separated from great black-hawk by its call, a series of "spinking" notes, quite high-pitched for a large bird. Pairs of common black-hawks often circle together; because females are noticeably larger than males, the male often goes down on checklists as common black-hawk and female as "obvious" great black-hawk. I've never seen great black-hawk in Trinidad.

Great black-hawk See previous species. Reported from heights of Blanchisseuse Road and over forested areas of Nariva Swamp. Common black-hawk has black tail with white band at base, whereas great black-hawk often appears to have white tail with black terminal band. Call a thin scream, reminiscent of red-tailed hawk.

Savanna hawk Agricultural Research Station, Wallerfield, Aripo Savannah, Mayaro Road (cattle ranch), and throughout central Trinidad. More common at low elevations than higher. ffrench considered it rare, but now more accurately described as locally common.

Black-collared hawk Rare, seen mostly along Mayaro Road (milepost 46 at boat trail to Bush Bush) and in Nariva Swamp. Wooded swamps.

Broad-winged hawk Uncommon but increasing in Trinidad; one of the most frequently seen raptors on Tobago.

Short-tailed hawk Overlooked although regular and widely distributed; often soars with vultures. Dark facial pattern resembles that of peregrine falcon.

White-tailed hawk Overlooked; distribution as previous species but more of a lowland species, less common in Northern Range. Hovers. As with previous species, dark facial pattern resembles that of peregrine falcon.

Zone-tailed hawk Overlooked or much more common than formerly, widespread; Heights of Aripo, Wallerfield, Mount St. Benedict, Nariva Swamp. Strongly resembles and mimics turkey vulture. Watch for "vulture" stooping on passing turkey vultures, from which it's easily distinguished (by use of binoculars) by bright yellow cere and feet; tail bands may be obscure. Often cruises just above treetops, against which background it's difficult to discern.

Ornate hawk-eagle Often nests on grounds of Asa Wright Nature Center and elsewhere in Arima Valley, where seen almost daily, especially before 9 am. (earlier than most other soaring raptors). Light underwings and narrow black tailbands distinguish it from locally common gray-headed kite, which has dark underwings and wide black tail bands.

Yellow-headed caracara Dramatic population increase in recent years; Caroni and Nariva Swamps, Wallerfield, Agricultural Research Station, Aripo Savannah. Unmistakable. No other raptor found in Trinidad or Tobago is creamy yellow with dark wings, striking pale patch in wing. Frequently pursued and harried by tropical kingbird.

116 **Merlin** Uncommon but regular visitor to both islands; widespread over open areas (sugarcane fields, swamps) where it pursues and

captures prey on the wing. Distinctive flight — about two deep wingbeats per second, almost no soaring or gliding; when in active pursuit of prey (often bats), wingbeats are so fast as to appear swallowlike.

Aplomado falcon Very rare; mostly along west coast, Caroni to Oropuche, also at Wallerfield and Nariva Swamp. Increasing number of reports, especially of individuals pursuing dickcissels in Nariva Swamp, may be a result of successful captive release program in Texas. Aplomado falcons follow dickcissels on migration.

Bat falcon Uncommon but regularly seen from overlooks along Blanchisseuse Road, Lalaja Road, upper Cumaca Road (on left just past Valencia), and Heights of Aripo as it dashes after bats and songbirds. Most easily seen dawn and dusk but active throughout day. Often perches at tip of tree top. Appears all black, flies like merlin.

Peregrine falcon Uncommon but regular visitor to both islands, widespread in open areas but particularly fond of mudflats, where it pursues its favorite prey, shorebirds; Caroni Swamp, Agricultural Research Station.

Common (Trinidad) piping-guan Extremely rare; small populations still found in the remote upper reaches of Northern Range, particularly Heights of Aripo, Cumaca, Matura; also in southeast (Trinity Hills). Stalk as you'd stalk wild turkey or grouse; call is weak, doesn't carry far, and is of little value in locating the bird. Sightings usually of solitary birds; occasional flocks of up to 6 seen.

Rails and crakes Generally difficult to observe because of habit of skulking on ground in dense vegetation, primarily in wetlands but also in grasslands. More common than realized. Learn calls from tapes, ffrench's descriptions, or firsthand and "list" far more by ear than by eye. Tape recorders with playback is best method for determining identity of mystery singers.

Clapper rail Easiest rail/crake to see because of large size and atypically nonsecretive behavior. Port-of-Spain Sewage Lagoons, along tidal creeks islandwide — prefers fiddler crabs as prey. Call, loud series of 3-8 grating notes — "kak, kak, kak" or "chek, chek, chek."

Gray-necked wood-rail Nariva and Caroni Swamps and around reservoirs at Pointe-à-Pierre Wild Fowl Trust, but rarely seen. Slightly larger than clapper rail, not likely to be mistaken for one. More secretive in Trinidad than in other parts of its range. See ffrench for description of call.

Rufous-necked wood-rail Very rarely seen or heard; only recent records are from El Socorro Marsh.

Sora Abundant winter visitor, El Socorro, Nariva, and Caroni Swamps.

Ash-throated crake Very rarely seen or heard; as with rufous-necked wood-rail, only recent records are from El Socorro Marsh.

Yellow-breasted crake Often the most abundant wetland species (except sora in winter). Marshes south of Caroni Swamp boat tour docks on Uriah Butler side of trail and El Socorro Marsh. Diagnostic marks — dark eyeline below pale eyestripe — must be noted quickly, before bird skulks back into vegetation. Call described as froglike, high-pitched double note accented on the first syllable, tee-di.

Spotted rail El Socorro Marsh; considered by local guides to be fairly common but difficult to observe except in early morning.

Purple gallinule Port-of-Spain Sewage Lagoons, Trincity Ponds. Uncommon, much less confiding than common moorhen, with which it shares habitat. Seeks cover when approached, hides in thick vegetation. Common in rice fields bordering Caroni Swamp, Nariva Swamp, and at South Oropuche.

Azure gallinule Also called azure-winged gallinule. Known only from a small colony in the Pumpkin Patch of south Nariva. In marsh vegetation on both sides of road just after it emerges from coconut plantation. Resembles immature purple gallinule but smaller. Often flies short distances.

Sungrebe Elusive and little-known species, frequents heavily forested areas around lakes, dams, streams in central Trinidad. Recent record of 4 birds at Hollis Dam.

Limpkin Uncommon; declining from hunting pressure. Frequents fresh water with large snails on which it feeds. Caroni and Nariva Swamps, rice fields near Caroni, marshes in southern Trinidad. More often heard than seen; ffrench's description apt — a loud, wailing scream, "krraow," often heard in background of jungle movies.

Southern lapwing Population explosion in recent years. Increasingly abundant at Agricultural Research Station, Wallerfield, Aripo Savannah, Nariva Swamp, Piarco Water Treatment Plant, Port-of-Spain Sewage Lagoons, and South Oropuche.

Plovers and sandpipers Caroni Swamp mudflats, Port-of-Spain Sewage Lagoons, Pointe-à-Pierre mudflats, Wallerfield; Buccoo Marsh, Tobago. Most North American species have been recorded; species range from abundant during migration to accidental at other times, some individuals (nonbreeders) remaining through summer. A telescope is invaluable for studying plumage details.

Collared plover Uncommon and local in season, Port-of-Spain Sewage Lagoons, Agricultural Research Station and other wet, grassy areas.

Wilson's plover Recent breeding record at Pointe-à-Pierre Wild Fowl Trust.

Gulls and terns In my experience the greatest concentrations of gulls and terns can be found at the Port-of-Spain Sewage Lagoons, the Trincity Ponds (terns only), Icacos Point in southwestern Trinidad, and in Turtle Bay, behind the Turtle Beach Hotel in Tobago.

Common black-headed gull Formerly regarded as accidental, now regular in small numbers at Port-of-Spain Sewage Lagoons and Turtle Bay, behind Turtle Beach Hotel, Tobago.

Sandwich tern Uncommon along coasts of both islands; commonly misidentified as Cayenne tern because bill of this race is entirely yellowish-orange, unlike yellow-tipped black bill of northern form. Both type breed in Netherlands Antilles (morphs of same species?). Watch for it resting on fishing boats behind the Turtle Beach Hotel, Tobago.

Roseate tern Uncommon but regular, only along northern coast of Trinidad and all coasts of Tobago.

Yellow-billed tern Piarco Water Treatment Plant, Trincity Ponds, Arena Dam, Port-of-Spain Sewage Lagoons; not much larger than least tern.

Bridled tern Common only along coast of Tobago; breeds on Little Tobago Island.

Sooty tern Abundant but only along coast of Tobago; breeds on Little Tobago Island.

Large-billed tern Same areas as yellow-billed tern; most common at Trincity Ponds, Port-of-Spain Sewage Lagoons, Caroni Swamp.

Brown noddy Abundant at times but only off Tobago; very few sightings from Trinidad. Breeds on Little Tobago Island.

Black skimmer Common but local; Port-of-Spain Sewage Lagoons and Pointe-à-Pierre dams.

Rock dove Not mentioned in ffrench or on many checklists (a "nonbird"), but conspicuous around barns; not so urban as in North America and Europe.

Pale-vented pigeon Uncommon and local in Trinidad; most easily seen in flight in Caroni Swamp after 4:30 pm. Size, shape, and flight style similar to rock dove. In Tobago can be found along road to Hillsborough Dam and on Old Castara Road.

Scaled pigeon Uncommon; Mount St. Benedict, Arima Valley; often seen flying across valleys in Northern Range. Wary; a telescope is useful for identifying distant birds exposed in treetops.

Band-tailed pigeon Rare; seen in heights, El Tucuche, Las Lapis Trace.

Eared dove Difficult to observe in Trinidad but common on Tobago; Crown Point Airport region, Pigeon Point, Kilgwyn Swamp.

Common ground-dove Uncommon and local; Agricultural Research Station (near cattle barns), Wallerfield, along Churchill-Roosevelt Highway on wires between Arima and Cumuto Road.

Plain-breasted ground-dove Nariva and in same areas as previous species; difficult to separate from it (see ffrench for details).

White-tipped dove Uncommon and rarely seen; call, "whooo", heard throughout day in Northern Range. Prefers drier regions than gray-fronted dove.

Blue-and-yellow macaw Extirpated; last stronghold was Nariva Swamp. Feral flock in northern Tobago near Charlotteville reduced to a lone bird by late 1992.

Red-bellied macaw Locally abundant; Nariva Swamp/Wallerfield flocks of more than 100. Frequents moriche and royal palms. Illegally hunted as cage bird (nest trees felled, young captured).

Green-rumped parrotlet Uncommon at higher elevations, more common in swamps and lowlands, singly or in small groups.

Lilac-tailed parrotlet Prefers higher elevations than previous species, especially rainforests; usually in flocks, sometimes large numbers. Inspect termitaria (termite structures) for silently feeding or nesting birds.

Scarlet-shouldered parrotlet Large flocks (40 birds) seen twice in recent years, once over Aripo Savannah (August 10) and once over Carapo, just west of Wallerfield (March 18).

Blue-headed parrot Prefers higher elevations than orange-winged. Common in Northern Range.

Yellow-crowned parrot Eastern side of Port-of-Spain and vicinity of University of the West Indies campus in Curepe. Introduced. Mentioned here because of the confused nature of its taxonomy. Both the AOU and Forshaw (**Parrots of the World**) use the name "yellow-headed parrot" to refer to *Amazona oratrix*, but the form (or species) thought to breed in Trinidad is the yellow-crowned parrot, *Amazona ochrocephala*, according to the AOU. Forshaw used the name "yellow-crowned parrot" for *ochrocephala* and other races, including *oratrix*. It appears that the name "yellow-headed parrot" pertains to the nominate form, *Amazona ochrocephala ochrocephala*.

Mangrove cuckoo Uncommon; mangroves along canals in Caroni Swamp and recently at Pigeon Point.

Dark-billed cuckoo Very rare, Caroni and Nariva Swamps.

Little cuckoo Uncommon and local; Wallerfield, Caroni Swamp. Skulks in lower branches. Responds to pishing.

Greater ani Uncommon; Nariva, Caroni, South Oropuche Swamps. Boatmen should be able to show it to you. Usually found in family groups of 4-7.

Common barn-owl Common, especially Diego Martin and Chaguaramas areas.

Spectacled owl Rare; most often found along Las Lapis Trace and in Chaguaramas area of northwestern Trinidad.

Short-tailed nighthawk Formerly called semicollared nighthawk. Apparently increasing; identify by low, erratic, bat-like flight (associates with bats). Hunts over marshes and forests; often seen at twilight along Blanchisseuse Road near Arima.

Nacunda nighthawk Rare; occasionally seen at dawn and dusk hawking flying insects over Wallerfield.

Common pauraque Uncommon; dawn and dusk at Wallerfield and near fire tower on Mount St. Benedict.

White-tailed nightjar Uncommon and usually silent; dawn and dusk over Blanchisseuse Road near Arima. In Tobago at Pigeon Point and Buccoo Marsh, roosts by day on mangrove roots.

Oilbird Rare and local; caves only. Best site is Asa Wright Nature Center. If closed, try Oropuche or Cumaca caves with local guide.

Common potoo Not uncommon on either island but camouflage renders it nearly invisible. Almost certain to be seen on boat trips in Caroni Swamp, spotted by use of spotlight after dark.

Chestnut-collared swift Uncommon; flies with other species of swifts over foothills and in heights. Nests at Asa Wright Nature Center at entrance to Oilbird cave.

White-collared swift Rare but large and conspicuous, especially at low elevations just before rain showers; at other times in heights. Large flocks of migrants pass over at limits of visibility.

***Chaetura* swifts** Four species, all a challenge to identify; try to view from above, noting size, shape, color of rump patch. ffrench provides good field marks.

Chapman's swift Least common *Chaetura* swift; difficult to identify even when seen from above. Best viewing spots are overlooks on Blanchisseuse Road between Textel entrance and Las Lapas Trace, Wallerfield at dawn or dusk.

Short-tailed swift *Chaetura* species seen most often, especially at lower elevations and over urban areas; similar to chimney swift.

Lesser swallow-tailed swift Rare but easily identified; most often reported over Mount St. Benedict.

Fork-tailed palm-swift Uncommon; frequents savannahs with moriche palms. Wallerfield, Aripo Savannah, Nariva Swamp, Port-of-Spain near Botanical Gardens.

White-tailed sabrewing Increasing in numbers since their nadir in early 1970s. Still extremely rare, Tobago only; Gilpin Trace. (I'd love to have a good photograph of this species.)

Brown violet-ear Rare; a few individuals frequent estate house on L'Orange Road north of Ruiz Trace (Heights of Aripo); infrequent at Asa Wright Nature Center. Often catches insects on the wing, a behavioral characteristic of possible identification value.

Blue-crowned motmot Uncommon in Trinidad, common and tame on Tobago. Look and listen ("hooooot") in Arena Forest.

Trogons Can be distinguished by calls, all of which are ventriloquial, given with closed beak. Collared is unique — short, 3-5 notes, starts loud then diminishes in volume. White-tailed is 10-20 notes; compare with violaceous, with about same number of notes given twice as fast.

Collared trogon Common but inconspicuous and highly ventriloquial; Blanchiseusse Road above Asa Wright Nature Center, other heights. Only trogon in Tobago, population increasing.

American pygmy-kingfisher Uncommon and inconspicuous but widespread, Bush Bush Creek, Damier River. Prefers small streams and tidal creeks, where it plunge-dives for minnows; also catches insects along streams.

Rufous-tailed jacamar Uncommon and elusive in Trinidad (Arena Forest, Mount St. Benedict), more often heard than seen; common and tame on Tobago.

Channel-billed toucan Common but often feeds in treetops, where difficult to spot; loud, raucous calls announce its presence. Northern Range, Arena Forest.

Crimson-crested woodpecker Rare; prefers lowland forests with large standing dead trees; sometimes seen in lower Arima Valley, Maridale Road.

Black-crested antshrike Uncommon; found in most swamps and Wallerfield seeps. Most active 1:30-3:30 pm when most other species are quiet.

Plain antvireo Uncommon; forest heights along Blanchisseuse and Lalaja Roads.

Silvered antbird Most likely at Bush Bush Creek bridge on Mayaro Road. Loud, long call rises up scale, then falls; responds quickly to taped playback.

White-bellied antbird Common but easily overlooked, forages on ground inforests; Arena forest. Woodpeckerlike calls confirm its presence.

Black-faced antthrush Widespread but elusive at middle to high elevations in rainforests; melancholy 4-note whistle can be heard throughout day. Easily attracted to whistled imitation of call.

Scaled antpitta Considered by local guides to be extirpated, but call notes heard in 1976 in Matura Forest in southeastern Trinidad. May still exist in the Northern Range.

Flycatchers Flycatchers fall into two groups — those that are easy to identify and those that are nearly impossible to identify.

Excluding unique great kiskadee, fork-tailed flycatcher, and the like, identification of members of this group should be based on physical characteristics in combination with call notes, especially for *Myiarchus* flycatchers. Many rare species seem more common in northeastern coastal scrub forests than elsewhere, except on islands between Trinidad and Venezuela (excluded from this guide).

Crested doradito Freshwater swamps bordering Caroni Swamp, all records June-Sept. Not in NE in hills around Salybia (Trinidad) as I previously believed.

Short-tailed pygmy-tyrant Rare along northeastern coast, in hills around Salybia on Saline Bay, in Arena Forest, and recent nesting at Asa Wright Nature Center low in tree.

White-throated spadebill Rare along northeastern coast, in hills around Salybia on Saline Bay, in Arena Forest, and throughout Central Range. Sits motionless for extended periods of time.

Bran-colored flycatcher Uncommon in lowlying areas such as Wallerfield.

Euler's flycatcher Fortunately (because species in the genus *Empidonax* are notoriously difficult to identify), the only *Empidonax* species in the islands; widespread.

Sulphury flycatcher Uncommon; prefers moriche palms at Wallerfield. Mewing call similar to that of smooth-billed ani.

Fork-tailed flycatcher Abundant in proper season, scarce at other times; noted here because roosts in enormous numbers in Caroni Swamp mangroves, flying in at twilight and leaving shortly after sunrise. Also occasional at Port-of-Spain sewage lagoons.

Bearded bellbird Uncommon but usually within earshot anywhere in Northern Range except late August through October; ventriloquial and difficult to spot. Accessible calling grounds on Asa Wright Nature Center property, along Blanchisseuse Road, Ruiz Trace (Heights of Aripo).

Golden-headed manakin Most abundant rainforest species, Trinidad only. Noted here because highly ventriloquial; when its distinctive, rifle-ricochet call "pit-tu" is heard, look twice the height of perceived perch to spot bird.

White-winged swallow Uncommon, in small numbers at Arena Dam, Wallerfield, sometimes Agricultural Research Station.

Blue-and-white swallow Uncommon, migrant in south Trinidad.

Hawks for insects over sugarcane fields; roosts in mangroves in southern Caroni Swamp.

Southern rough-winged swallow Common; differs from northern rough-winged swallow primarily by conspicuous apricot-colored rump. Wallerfield, Blanchisseuse, Piarco Water Treatment Plant.

Greater bird-of-paradise Formerly resident, introduced from Aru Islands off New Guinea. Hard hit by Hurricane Flora in 1963. No sightings in recent years. Undoubtedly extirpated.

Tropical house-wren Abundant, particularly around human habitation; mentioned here because differs significantly enough to be split again from "generic" house-wren. Song and coloration of tropical house-wren is distinctly different from that of its northern counterparts. It's cinnamon, not gray-brown.

Long-billed gnatwren Common and widespread but elusive in understory, where dry, monotone trill announces presence.

Thrushes As group much more active and vocal in evening than in morning. Most prefer middle to high elevations.

Orange-billed nightingale-thrush Very rare and regarded as extremely secretive. Found in the highest points only — Heights of Aripo and El Tucuche.

Chivi vireo Common but status uncertain; regarded by some as race of red-eyed vireo, which it strongly resembles in appearance, song, and behavior.

North American warblers Many species seen from once to many times, often in strikingly dissimilar habitats than those utilized for nesting. Usually silent on wintering grounds. Species most likely to be seen include yellow (perhaps Caribbean race), northern waterthrush (abundant), American redstart (common), blackpoll, black-and-white, and prothonotary.

Common yellowthroat Status unclear because of similarity with the following species, from which it can be told by brown (not gray) crown and black mask extending well (not just very narrowly) above bill.

Masked yellowthroat See previous species. Rare but probably more common than records would indicate. Found in same grassy and marshy habitats as preferred by common yellowthroat.

Golden-crowned warbler Common but often overlooked in low to middle story of rainforest. Most frequently seen along

Blanchisseuse Road above Asa Wright Nature Center. Song weak, nondescript; of little value in locating bird.

Bicolored conebill Uncommon and local; most easily seen in mangroves along banks of canals in Caroni Swamp; also possible along Nariva River (Mayaro Road) and Bush Bush Creek. Chatters.

Speckled tanager Uncommon; small flocks, prefers heights; above Asa Wright Nature Center on Blanchisseuse Road, Andrews Trace.

Golden-rumped euphonia In hills above Mount St. Benedict.

Trinidad euphonia Rare and local because of trapping for use as cagebird; regularly seen in Arima Valley, particularly at Simla. Elsewhere most easily seen in Central Range.

Blue-capped tanager Rare; prefers higher elevations; above Asa Wright Nature Center along Blanchisseuse Road, Heights of Aripo.

Red-crowned ant-tanager Not uncommon but difficult to view; darts away rather than investigating pishing or owl calls. Along trail to Dunstan (Oilbird) Cave at Asa Wright Nature Center, also near wooden bridge just before Hollis Dam (north of Valencia).

Swallow-Tanager Rare; prefers treetops in forest heights; Andrew's Trace, Heights of Aripo.

Streaked saltator Very rare except in extreme northwestern Trinidad (west of Chaguaramas) in dry brush.

Red-capped cardinal Rare and elusive; looks like small thrush. Caroni Swamp (boat trips), Pointe-à-Pierre Wild Fowl Trust.

Seedeaters Most species rare and decreasing rapidly. Trapping has sadly reduced numbers of finches except for mediocre singers such as blue-black and black-faced grassquits. Plum Mitan Road can be good for seedeaters.

Saffron finch Common but local, especially in suburban areas near Pointe-à-Pierre; sometimes seen in Port-of-Spain at Botanical Gardens.

Giant cowbird Common but local; Agricultural Research Station, Aripo Savannah, Wallerfield. Strongly resembles common grackle in size and flight style.

Moriche oriole Rarely seen; Aripo Savannah, Nariva Swamp; about one sighting every six months. Prefers moriche palms with fruiting figs nearby.

ACCIDENTAL OR EXCEPTIONALLY RARE SPECIES

Recorded for Trinidad or Tobago but never to be expected.

Bulwer's petrel
Cory's shearwater
Manx shearwater
Sooty shearwater
Wilson's storm-petrel
White-tailed tropicbird
Northern gannet
Masked booby
Gray heron
Reddish egret
Chestnut-bellied heron
White ibis
Jabiru stork
Wood stork
Greater flamingo
Horned screamer
Snow goose
Mallard
Northern shoveler
Muscovy duck
Comb duck
Green-winged teal
Southern pochard
Ring-necked duck
Lesser yellow-headed vulture
Black-collared hawk
Rufous crab-hawk
Snail kite
Swainson's hawk
Black hawk-eagle
Crested caracara
Aplomado falcon
Orange-breasted falcon
Burrowing owl
Ash-throated crake
Paint-billed crake

Caribbean coot
American coot
Sungrebe
Double-striped thick-knee
Wilson's phalarope
Snowy plover
Common ringed-plover
American oystercatcher
American avocet
Common greenshank
Spotted redshank
Baird's sandpiper
Eskimo curlew
Long-billed curlew
Marbled godwit
Ruff
South Polar skua
Lesser black-backed gull
Sabine's gull
Herring gull
Caspian tern
Lesser noddy
Fairy tern
Scaled dove
Scarlet macaw
Red-shouldered macaw
Scarlet-shouldered parrotlet
Monk parakeet
Yellow-crowned parrot
Black-billed cuckoo
Common nighthawk
Black swift
Rufous-shafted woodstar
Amazon kingfisher
Scaled antpitta
Small-billed elaenia

Spotted tody-flycatcher
Variegated flycatcher
Crested doradito
White bellbird
Cliff swallow
White wagtail
Gray-cheeked thrush
Veery
Yellow-throated vireo
Golden-winged warbler
Northern parula
Chestnut-sided warbler
Magnolia warbler
Black-throated blue warbler
Yellow-rumped warbler
Black-throated green warbler
Blackburnian warbler
Prairie warbler
Bay-breasted warbler
Ovenbird

Common yellowthroat
Hooded warbler
Canada warbler
Golden-rumped euphonia
Indigo bunting
Gray seedeater
Slate-colored seedeater
Variable seedeater
Lesson's seedeater
Yellow-bellied seedeater
Large-billed seed-finch
Orange-fronted yellow-finch
Scarlet tanager
Rose-breasted grosbeak
Red-winged blackbird
Troupial
Northern oriole
Bobolink
Red siskin

Black-tailed tityra, by Don R. Eckelberry

MISCELLANEOUS INFORMATION

Useful Conversions

> 1 meter = 3.3 feet
> 1 foot = 0.3 meters
> 1 mile = 1.6 kilometers
> 1 kilometer = 0.62 miles

Laws Pertaining to Birds on Trinidad and Tobago

The following birds are classified as game birds. Daily bag limits are 30 ducks and five night-herons per person.

Neotropic cormorant
Double-crested cormorant (designated although as yet never
  recorded from either island!)
Great blue heron
Cocoi heron
Black-crowned night-heron
Yellow-crowned night-heron
Boat-billed heron
Black-bellied whistling-duck
All ducks except white-cheeked pintail and muscovy
Black vulture
All rallids (coots, rails, etc.)
All plovers
All scolopacids (snipes, curlews, sandpipers, yellowlegs,
  godwits, etc.)
All pigeons
Orange-winged parrot

The following birds may be captured or kept captive by cage providing not less than one cubic foot per captive bird:

Green-rumped parrotlet, Trinidad euphonia, violaceous euphonia, gray seedeater, Lesson's seedeater, yellow-bellied seedeater, lesser seed-finch.

The following birds are declared vermin:

Crested oropendola, orange-winged parrot, rufous-vented chachalaca

A SNORKELERS' GUIDE TO THE BAY AT ARNOS VALE, TOBAGO

[The following narrative is reproduced here, with slight modification, by the kind permission of Tom and Katharine Almy of Etna, New Hampshire, USA. It has been of great value to those of us who snorkel in Arnos Vale Bay.]

After twenty trips to the Caribbean and three to Arnos Vale, we are firm in our belief that one of the purest joys in the Western world is snorkeling and that one of the top two or three choices for the *ideal* site is Arnos Vale Bay.

We confess that this choice is dictated in part by very personal considerations. The riot of flowers, the tanagers and motmots, the excellent rum punches, and the *cordon bleu* cookery appeal to us so much that we may be viewing the local seascape through rose-colored faceplates. But we are just moderately good swimmers. We want our coral and our fish within a hundred yards or so of the beach; we dislike spending all day in a bobbing launch to reach a distant reef. We have settled for the snorkel and have not ventured into scuba technique and deep-water. And our interest in meeting sharks and barracudas would have to grow to be even cursory. So Arnos Vale suits us fine.

Over the years we seem to have acquired a modest familiarity with the ecology of the coral reef; we lag miles behind the experts. Nevertheless, we have found, over after-dinner coffee on the terrace, that there are visitors to Arnos Vale, certainly as capable as we (who are approaching our sixtieth birthdays) of venturing into the lovely world that lies just offshore and who could benefit by a simple chart and a little advice. The really experienced snorkeler may be either bored or mildly amused at what we have to offer, but perhaps others will find this useful.

When the water in the bay is calm, the snorkeler can go anywhere. When the bay is rough and the wind strong, waves of great force come down the center, sparing the two sides. Because the height of *gaucherie* is to be dashed on a jagged coral, we always feel comfortable entering the water along the boat channel on the left (west) side, which also serves for the landing of small fishing boats. To the left is an area we estimate at 2-5 feet deep and which is to be avoided or entered with caution when waves are large. Yet when the water is calm, the clarity of the water plus the nearness of the fish make beautiful sights. Just outside this zone, on the edge of far deeper water, is a forest of antler coral (or elkhorn coral) whose broad brown branches frequently harbor large schools of blue-striped grunts, swaying gracefully in rhythm with the surge.

But our "all-weather" route carries us out the boat channel, curves to the right at the edge of the "elkhorn" zone, keeps well inside the exposed rocks, and leads us through calmer water into a series of underwater bays at the far right (eastern) side. These bays are lined by steep coral cliffs, have an irregular stony bottom, and are 10-30 feet deep. Features of this area include a number of large masses of star coral, rounded or roughly conical in shape, and colored gray, lavender, brown, or pale green according to the covering of algae. In some places the star coral reaches to within three feet or so of the surface. These masses, as well as the edges of the "cliffs," have been the most rewarding sites of all for the observation of various species of fish.

The commoner species you will meet are the multicolored parrot-fish, the doctor fish and the blue tang (often in schools), damselfish of all sizes and colors, blue-striped grunts, sergeant majors, and blue-minnows. Less common but fairly dependable treats are the queen and French angelfish, butterflyfish , squirrelfish, trunkfish, triggerfish , and trumpetfish. On occasion we have seen such wonders as a really huge (three-foot) brilliant blue parrotfish, some yellowtails chasing a tremendous school of four-inch silversides, a small turtle, an octopus, and (at a distance) a green moray eel. Aside from elkhorn, stinging coral, and star coral, the cove abounds in sea fans, sea whips, and multicolored sponges. You may have to share the bay with fishing pelicans, but you're bigger than they are, and there's plenty of room.

In case you did not know it, some corals sting very painfully when touched, all corals are rough enough to produce a nasty abrasion (which heals slowly) when bumped hard, and sea urchin spines are nasty things that must be removed surgically. All of the fish are slimy, and some (like the doctorfish) have sharp spines. We're probably fainthearted, but our rules are:

1. *Don't touch anything,* if possible.

2. Walk into the water buffeted by the waves while standing on one foot.

3. Always wear fins that cover the entire foot, including the heel. Use them and nothing else to push away from a coral surface.

4. Make most adjustments of face mask and snorkel while treading water. If it is necessary to stand on coral, pick a good, flat surface with minimal wave action.

Other people are much more daring than we and nevertheless seem to live out a good life. But within the conservative limits mentioned above, we have had a pleasant sense of adventure, renewed annually or nearly so, and few scratches to show for it. We wish you no less.

SCIENTIFIC AND COMMON NAMES OF THE BIRDS OF TRINIDAD AND TOBAGO

TINAMOU
Little tinamou   *Crypturellus soui*

GREBES
Least grebe   *Tachybaptus dominicus*
Pied-billed grebe   *Podilymbus podiceps*

SHEARWATERS & PETRELS
✓ Bulwer's petrel   *Bulweria bulwerii*
Cory's shearwater   *Calonectris diomedea*
Great shearwater   *Puffinus gravis*
Manx shearwater   *Puffinus puffinus*
Sooty shearwater   *Puffinus griseus*
Audubon's shearwater   *Puffinus lherminieri*
Leach's storm-petrel   *Oceanodroma leucorhoa*
Wilson's storm-petrel   *Oceanites oceanicus*

TROPICBIRD
Red-billed tropicbird   *Phaethon aethereus*
White-tailed tropicbird   *Phaethon lepturus*

BOOBIES
Masked booby   *Sula dactylatra*
Brown booby   *Sula leucogaster*
✓ Red-footed booby   *Sula sula*
Northern gannet   *Morus bassanus*

PELICAN
Brown pelican   *Pelecanus occidentalis*

CORMORANT
Neotropic cormorant   *Phalacrocorax olivaceus*

ANHINGA
Anhinga   *Anhinga anhinga*

FRIGATEBIRD
Magnificent frigatebird   *Fregata magnificens*

BITTERNS & HERONS
Gray heron   *Ardea cinerea*
Great blue heron   *Ardea herodias*

Cocoi heron	*Ardea cocoi*
Great egret	*Casmerodius albus*
Little egret	*Egretta garzetta*
Western reef-heron	*Egretta gularis*
Snowy egret	*Egretta thula*
Little blue heron	*Egretta caerulea*
Tricolored heron	*Egretta tricolor*
Reddish egret	*Egretta rufescens*
Green heron	*Butorides striatus*
Striated heron	*Butorides virescens*
Chestnut-bellied heron	*Agamia agami*
Cattle egret	*Bubulcus ibis*
Black-crowned night-heron	*Nycticorax nycticorax*
Yellow-crowned night-heron	*Nycticorax violaceus*
Rufescent tiger-heron	*Tigrisoma lineatum*
✓ Stripe-backed bittern	*Ixobrychus involucris*
Least bittern	*Ixobrychus exilis*
Pinnated bittern	*Botaurus pinnatus*
Boat-billed heron	*Cochlearius cochlearius*

STORKS
Jabiru stork	*Jabiru mycteria*
Wood stork	*Mycteria americana*

IBISES & SPOONBILL
White ibis	*Eudocimus albus*
Scarlet ibis	*Eudocimus ruber*
Glossy ibis	*Plegadis falcinellus*
Roseate spoonbill	*Ajaia ajaja*

FLAMINGO
Greater flamingo	*Phoenicopterus ruber*

SCREAMER
Horned screamer	*Anhima cornuta*

DUCKS & GEESE
Fulvous whistling-duck	*Dendrocygna bicolor*
✓ White-faced whistling-duck	*Dendrocygna viduata*
Black-bellied whistling-duck	*Dendrocygna autumnalis*
Snow goose	*Chen caerulescens*
Mallard	*Anas platyrhynchas*
Green-winged teal	*Anas crecca*
American wigeon	*Anas americana*
White-cheeked pintail	*Anas bahamensis*
Blue-winged teal	*Anas discors*
Northern shoveler	*Anas clypeata*
✓ Southern pochard	*Netta erythrophthalma*
Lesser scaup	*Aythya affinis*
Ring-necked duck	*Aythya collaris*
Comb duck	*Sarkidiornis melanotos*
Muscovy duck	*Cairina moschata*
Masked duck	*Oxyura dominica*

NEW WORLD VULTURES
King vulture	*Sarcoramphus papa*
Black vulture	*Coragyps atratus*
Turkey vulture	*Cathartes aura*
Lesser yellow-headed vulture	*Cathartes burrovianus*

KITES, HAWKS & EAGLES
White-tailed kite	*Elanus leucurus*
Pearl kite	*Gampsonyx swainsonii*
American swallow-tailed kite	*Elanoides forficatus*

Gray-headed kite	*Leptodon cayanensis*
Hook-billed kite	*Chondrohierax uncinatus*
Double-toothed kite	*Harpagus bidentatus*
Plumbeous kite	*Ictinia plumbea*
Snail kite	*Rostrhamus sociabilis*
White-tailed hawk	*Buteo albicaudatus*
Zone-tailed hawk	*Buteo albonotatus*
Broad-winged hawk	*Buteo platypterus*
Short-tailed hawk	*Buteo brachyurus*
Swainson's hawk	*Buteo swainsoni*
Gray hawk	*Buteo nitidus*
White hawk	*Leucopternis albicollis*
Black-collared hawk	*Busarellus nigricollis*
Savanna hawk	*Buteogallus meridionalis*
Common black-hawk	*Buteogallus anthracinus*
⌐ Rufous crab-hawk	*Buteogallus aequinoctialis*
Great black-hawk	*Buteogallus urubitinga*
Ornate hawk-eagle	*Spizaetus ornatus*
Black hawk-eagle	*Spizaetus tyrannus*
Long-winged harrier	*Circus buffoni*

OSPREY
Osprey	*Pandion haliaetus*

CARACARAS & FALCONS
Yellow-headed caracara	*Milvago chimachima*
Crested caracara	*Polyborus plancus*
Peregrine falcon	*Falco peregrinus*
Orange-breasted falcon	*Falco dieroleucus*
Bat falcon	*Falco rufigularis*
Aplomado falcon	*Falco femoralis*
Merlin	*Falco columbarius*
American kestrel	*Falco sparverius*

CHACHALACA & GUAN
Rufous-vented chachalaca	*Ortalis ruficauda*
⌐ Common piping-guan	*Aburria pipile*

LIMPKIN
Limpkin	*Aramus guarauna*

CRAKES, RAILS, GALLINULES, & COOT
Clapper rail	*Rallus longirostris*
h Spotted rail	*Pardirallus maculatus*
Gray-necked wood-rail	*Aramides cajanea*
Rufous-necked wood-rail	*Aramides axillaris*
Sora	*Porzana carolina*
⌐ Ash-throated crake	*Porzana albicollis*
h Yellow-breasted crake	*Porzana flaviventer*
⌐ Gray-breasted crake	*Laterallus exilis*
⌐ Paint-billed crake	*Neocrex erythrops*
Common moorhen	*Gallinula chloropus*
Purple gallinule	*Porphyula martinica*
Azure gallinule	*Porphyrula flavirostris*
Caribbean coot	*Fulica caribaea*
American coot	*Fulica americana*

SUNGREBE
Sungrebe	*Heliornis fulica*

JACANA
Wattled jacana	*Jacana jacana*

134

OYSTERCATCHER
American oystercatcher   *Haematopus palliatus*

THICK-KNEE
Double-striped thick-knee   *Burhinus bistriatus*

PLOVERS
Southern lapwing   *Vanellus chilensis*
Black-bellied plover   *Pluvialis squatarola*
Lesser golden-plover   *Pluvialis dominica*
Common ringed-plover   *Charadrius hiaticula*
Semipalmated plover   *Charadrius semipalmatus*
Snowy plover   *Charadrius alexandrinus*
Collared plover   *Charadrius collaris*
Killdeer   *Charadrius vociferus*
Wilson's plover   *Charadrius wilsonia*

SANDPIPERS & ALLIES
Ruddy turnstone   *Arenaria interpres*
Solitary sandpiper   *Tringa solitaria*
Lesser yellowlegs   *Tringa flavipes*
Greater yellowlegs   *Tringa melanoleuca*
Common greenshank   *Tringa nebularis*
Spotted redshank   *Tringa erythropus*
Spotted sandpiper   *Actitis macularis*
Willet   *Catoptrophorus semipalmatus*
Red knot   *Calidris canutus*
Least sandpiper   *Calidris minutilla*
White-rumped sandpiper   *Calidris fuscicollis*
Baird's sandpiper   *Calidris bairdii*
Pectoral sandpiper   *Calidris melanotos*
Semipalmated sandpiper   *Calidris pusilla*
Western sandpiper   *Calidris mauri*
Sanderling   *Calidris alba*
Stilt sandpiper   *Calidris himantopus*
Ruff   *Philomachus pugnax*
Buff-breasted sandpiper   *Tryngites subruficollis*
Upland sandpiper   *Bartramia longicauda*
Whimbrel   *Numenius phaeopus*
✓ Eskimo curlew   *Numenius borealis*
Long-billed curlew   *Numenius americanus*
Hudsonian godwit   *Limosa haemastica*
Marbled godwit   *Limosa fedoa*
Short-billed dowitcher   *Limnodromus griseus*
Common snipe   *Gallinago gallinago*

PHALAROPE
Wilson's phalarope   *Phalaropus tricolor*

STILT & AVOCET
Black-necked stilt   *Himantopus mexicanus*
American avocet   *Recurvirostra americana*

JAEGERS & SKUA
Pomarine jaeger   *Stercorarius pomarinus*
Parasitic jaeger   *Stercorarius parasiticus*
South Polar skua   *Catharacta maccormicki*

GULLS & TERNS
Herring gull   *Larus argentatus*
Lesser black-backed gull   *Larus fuscus*
Ring-billed gull   *Larus delawarensis*
Laughing gull   *Larus atricilla*
Common black-headed gull   *Larus ridibundus*

135

Sabine's gull	*Xema sabini*
Black tern	*Chlidonias niger*
Large-billed tern	*Phaetusa simplex*
Gull-billed tern	*Sterna nilotica*
Caspian tern	*Sterna caspia*
Common tern	*Sterna hirundo*
Roseate tern	*Sterna dougallii*
Bridled tern	*Sterna anaethetus*
Sooty tern	*Sterna fuscata*
Yellow-billed tern	*Sterna superciliaris*
Least tern	*Sterna antillarum*
Royal tern	*Sterna maxima*
Sandwich tern	*Sterna sandvicensis*
Brown noddy	*Anous stolidus*
✓ Lesser noddy	*Anous tenuirostris*
✓ Fairy tern	*Gygis alba*

SKIMMER
Black skimmer	*Rynchops niger*

DOVES & PIGEONS
Rock dove	*Columba livia*
Band-tailed pigeon	*Columba fasciata*
Scaled pigeon	*Columba speciosa*
Pale-vented pigeon	*Columba cayennensis*
Eared dove	*Zenaida auriculata*
Common ground-dove	*Columbina passerina*
Plain-breasted ground-dove	*Columbina minuta*
Ruddy ground-dove	*Columbina talpacoti*
Blue ground-dove	*Claravis pretiosa*
Scaled dove	*Columbina squammata*
White-tipped dove	*Leptotila verreauxi*
Gray-fronted dove	*Leptotila rufaxilla*
Ruddy quail-dove	*Geotrygon montana*
Lined quail-dove	*Geotrygon linearis*

MACAWS, PARROTLETS, & PARROTS
Monk parakeet	*Myiopsitta monachus*
Blue-and-yellow macaw	*Ara ararauna*
Scarlet macaw	*Ara macao*
Red-bellied macaw	*Ara manilata*
Red-shouldered macaw	*Ara nobilis*
Green-rumped parrotlet	*Forpus passerinus*
Lilac-tailed parrotlet	*Touit batavica*
Scarlet-shouldered parrotlet	*Touit huetii*
Blue-headed parrot	*Pionus menstruus*
Yellow-crowned parrot	*Amazona ochrocephala*
Orange-winged parrot	*Amazona amazonica*

CUCKOOS
Black-billed cuckoo	*Coccyzus erythropthalmus*
Yellow-billed cuckoo	*Coccyzus americanus*
Mangrove cuckoo	*Coccyzus minor*
? Dark-billed cuckoo	*Coccyzus melacoryphus*
Squirrel cuckoo	*Piaya cayana*
Little cuckoo	*Piaya minuta*
Greater ani	*Crotophaga major*
Smooth-billed ani	*Crotophaga ani*
Striped cuckoo	*Tapera naevia*

BARN-OWL
Common barn-owl	*Tyto alba*

OWLS

Tropical screech-owl	*Otus choliba*
Spectacled owl	*Pulsatrix perspicillata*
Ferruginous pygmy-owl	*Glaucidium brasilianum*
Burrowing owl	*Athene cunicularia*
Mottled owl	*Ciccaba virgata*
Striped owl	*Asio clamator*

OILBIRD

Oilbird	*Steatornis caripensis*

POTOO

Common potoo	*Nyctibius griseus*

GOATSUCKERS

Short-tailed nighthawk	*Lurocalis semitorquatus*
Lesser nighthawk	*Chordeiles acutipennis*
Common nighthawk	*Chordeiles minor*
Nacunda nighthawk	*Podager nacunda*
Common pauraque	*Nyctidromus albicollis*
Rufous nightjar	*Caprimulgus rufus*
White-tailed nightjar	*Caprimulgus cayennensis*

SWIFTS

White-collared swift	*Streptoprocne zonaris*
Chestnut-collared swift	*Cypseloides rutilus*
Black swift	*Cypseloides niger*
Chapman's swift	*Chaetura chapmani*
Gray-rumped swift	*Chaetura cinereiventris*
Band-rumped swift	*Chaetura spinicauda*
Short-tailed swift	*Chaetura brachyura*
Lesser swallow-tailed swift	*Panyptila cayennensis*
Fork-tailed palm-swift	*Reinarda squamata*

HUMMINGBIRDS

Rufous-breasted hermit	*Glaucis hirsuta*
Green hermit	*Phaethornis guy*
Little hermit	*Phaethornis loguemareus*
White-tailed sabrewing	*Campylopterus ensipennis*
White-necked jacobin	*Florisuga mellivora*
Brown violet-ear	*Colibri delphinae*
Green-throated mango	*Anthracothorax viridugula*
Black-throated mango	*Anthracothorax nigricollis*
Ruby-topaz hummingbird	*Chrysolampis mosquitus*
Tufted coquette	*Lophornis ornata*
Blue-chinned sapphire	*Chlorestes notatus*
Blue-tailed emerald	*Chlorostilbon mellisugus*
White-tailed goldenthroat	*Polytmus guainumbi*
White-chested emerald	*Amazilia chionopectus*
Copper-rumped hummingbird	*Amazilia tobaci*
Long-billed starthroat	*Heliomaster longirostris*
Rufous-shafted woodstar	*Chaetocercus jourcanii*

TROGONS

White-tailed trogon	*Trogon viridis*
Collared trogon	*Trogon collaris*
Violaceous trogon	*Trogon violaceus*

KINGFISHERS

Ringed kingfisher	*Ceryle torquata*
Belted kingfisher	*Ceryle alcyon*
Amazon kingfisher	*Chloroceryle amazona*
Green kingfisher	*Chloroceryle americana*
American pygmy-kingfisher	*Chloroceryle aenea*

137

MOTMOT
Blue-crowned motmot   *Motmotus momota*

JACAMAR
Rufous-tailed jacamar   *Galbula ruficauda*

TOUCAN
Channel-billed toucan   *Ramphastos vitellinus*

WOODPECKERS
Golden-olive woodpecker   *Piculus rubiginosus*
Chestnut woodpecker   *Celeus elegans*
Lineated woodpecker   *Dryocopus lineatus*
Red-crowned woodpecker   *Melanerpes rubricapillus*
Red-rumped woodpecker   *Veniliornis kirkii*
Crimson-crested woodpecker   *Campephilus melanoleucos*

WOODCREEPERS
Plain-brown woodcreeper   *Dendrocincla fuliginosa*
Olivaceous woodcreeper   *Sittasomus griseicapillus*
Straight-billed woodcreeper   *Xiphorhynchus picus*
Buff-throated woodcreeper   *Xiphorhynchus guttatus*
Streak-headed woodcreeper   *Lepidocolaptes souleyetii*

SPINETAILS & ALLIES
Pale-breasted spinetail   *Synallaxis albescens*
Stripe-breasted spinetail   *Synallaxis cinnamomea*
Yellow-chinned spinetail   *Certhiaxis cinnamomea*
Steaked xenops   *Xenops rutilans*
Gray-throated leaftosser   *Sclerurus albigularis*

ANTBIRDS
Great antshrike   *Taraba major*
Black-crested antshrike   *Sakesphorus canadensis*
Barred antshrike   *Thamnophilus doliatus*
Plain antvireo   *Dysithamnus mentalis*
White-flanked antwren   *Myrmotherula axillaris*
White-fringed antwren   *Formicivora grisea*
Silvered antbird   *Sclateria naevia*
White-bellied antbird   *Myrmeciza longipes*
Black-faced antthrush   *Formicarius analis*
Scaled antpitta   *Grallaria guatimalensis*

COTINGAS
White bellbird   *Procnias alba*
Bearded bellbird   *Procnias averano*

MANAKINS
Golden-headed manakin   *Pipra erythrocephala*
White-bearded manakin   *Manacus manacus*
Blue-backed manakin   *Chiroxiphia lanceolata*

TYRANT-FLYCATCHERS
Pied water-tyrant   *Fluvicola pica*
White-headed marsh-tyrant   *Fluvicola leucocephala*
Bright-rumped attila   *Attila spadeceus*
Fork-tailed flycatcher   *Tyrannus savana*
Tropical kingbird   *Tyrannus melancholicus*
Gray kingbird   *Tyrannus dominicensis*
Sulphury flycatcher   *Tyrannopsis sulphurea*
Variegated flycatcher   *Empidonomus varius*
Piratic flycatcher   *Legatus leucophaius*
Boat-billed flycatcher   *Megarynchus pitangua*
Streaked flycatcher   *Myiodynastes maculatus*
138 Great kiskadee   *Pitangus sulphuratus*

Brown-crested flycatcher	*Myiarchus tyrannulus*
Venezuelan flycatcher	*Myiarchus venezuelensis*
Swainson's flycatcher	*Myiarchus swainsoni*
Dusky-capped flycatcher	*Myiarchus tuberculifer*
Olive-sided flycatcher	*Contopus borealis*
Tropical pewee	*Conotopus cinereus*
Euler's flycatcher	*Empidonax euleri*
Fuscous flycatcher	*Cnemotriccus fuscatus*
Bran-colored flycatcher	*Myiophobus fasciatus*
White-throated spadebill	*Platyrinchus mystaceus*
Yellow-olive flycatcher	*Tolmomyias sulphurescens*
Yellow-breasted flycatcher	*Tolmomyias flaviventris*
Spotted tody-flycatcher	*Todirostrum maculatum*
Short-tailed pygmy-tyrant	*Myiornis atricapillus*
Crested doradito	*Pseudocolapteryx sclateri*
Yellow-bellied elaenia	*Elaenia flavogaster*
Small-billed elaenia	*Elaenia parvirostris*
Lesser elaenia	*Elaenia chiriquensis*
Forest elaenia	*Myiopagis gaimardii*
Scrub flycatcher	*Sublegatus modestus*
Mouse-colored tyrannulet	*Phaeomyias murina*
Southern beardless-tyrannulet	*Camptostoma obsoletum*
Slaty-capped flycatcher	*Leptopogon superciliaris*
Olive-striped flycatcher	*Mionectes olivaceus*
Ochre-bellied flycatcher	*Mionectes oleagineus*
White-winged becard	*Pachyramphus polychopterus*
Black-tailed tityra	*Tityra cayana*

SWALLOWS

White-winged swallow	*Tachycineta albiventer*
Caribbean martin	*Progne dominicensis*
Gray-breasted martin	*Progne chalybea*
Blue-and-white swallow	*Pygochelidon cyanoleuca.*
Southern rough-winged swallow	*Stelgidopteryx ruficollis*
Bank swallow	*Riparia riparia*
Barn swallow	*Hirundo rustica*
Cliff swallow	*Hirundo pyrrhonota*

WAGTAIL

White wagtail	*Motacilla alba*

BIRD-OF-PARADISE

Greater bird-of-paradise	*Paradisea apoda*

WRENS

Rufous-breasted wren	*Thryothorus rutilus*
Tropical house-wren	*Troglodytes aedon*

MOCKINGBIRD

Tropical mockingbird	*Mimus gilvus*

GNATWREN & THRUSHES

Long-billed gnatwren	*Ramphocaenus melanurus*
Orange-billed nightingale-thrush	*Catharus aurantiirostris*
Gray-cheeked thrush	*Catharus minimus*
Veery	*Catharus fuscescens*
Yellow-legged thrush	*Platycichla flavipes*
Cocoa thrush	*Turdus fumigatus*
Bare-eyed thrush	*Turdus nudigenis*
White-necked thrush	*Turdus albicollis*

VIREOS & ALLIES

Rufous-browed peppershrike	*Cyclarhis gujanensis*
Yellow-throated vireo	*Vireo flavifrons*

Chivi vireo	*Vireo (olivaceus) chivi*
Black-whiskered vireo	*Vireo altiloquus*
Golden-fronted greenlet	*Hylophilus aurantiifrons*
Scrub greenlet	*Hylophilus flavipes*

ICTERIDS

Shiny cowbird	*Molothrus bonariensis*
Giant cowbird	*Scaphidura oryzivora*
Crested oropendola	*Psarocolius decumanus*
Yellow-rumped cacique	*Cacicus cela*
Carib grackle	*Quiscalus lugubris*
Yellow-hooded blackbird	*Agelaius icterocephalus*
Red-winged blackbird	*Agelaius phoeniceus*
Moriche oriole	*Icterus chrysocephalus*
Troupial	*Icterus icterus*
Yellow oriole	*Icterus nigrogularis*
Northern oriole	*Icterus galbula*
Red-breasted blackbird	*Sturnella militaris*
Bobolink	*Dolichonyx oryzivorus*

WOOD WARBLERS

Golden-winged warbler	*Vermivora chrysoptera*
Black-and-white warbler	*Mniotilta varia*
Prothonotary warbler	*Protonotaria citrea*
Northern parula	*Parula americana*
Tropical parula	*Parula pitiayumi*
Yellow warbler	*Dendroica petechia*
Magnolia warbler	*Dendroica magnolia*
Cape May warbler	*Dendroica tigrina*
Black-throated blue warbler	*Dendroica caerulescens*
Yellow-rumped warbler	*Dendroica coronata*
Black-throated green warbler	*Dendroica virens*
Prairie warbler	*Dendroica discolor*
Blackburnian warbler	*Dendroica fusca*
Chestnut-sided warbler	*Dendroica pensylvanica*
Bay-breasted warbler	*Dendroica castanea*
Blackpoll warbler	*Dendroica striata*
Ovenbird	*Seiurus aurocapillus*
Northern waterthrush	*Seiurus noveboracensis*
Common yellowthroat	*Geothlypis trichas*
Masked yellowthroat	*Geothlypis aequinoctialis*
Canada warbler	*Wilsonia canadensis*
Hooded warbler	*Wilsonia citrina*
American redstart	*Setophaga ruticilla*
Golden-crowned warbler	*Basileuterus culicivorus*

BANANAQUIT

Bananaquit	*Coereba flaveola*

SWALLOW-TANAGER

Swallow-Tanager	*Tersina viridis*

HONEYCREEPERS & TANAGERS

Bicolored conebill	*Conirostrum bicolor*
Purple honeycreeper	*Cyanerpes caeruleus*
Red-legged honeycreeper	*Cyanerpes cyaneus*
Green honeycreeper	*Chlorophanes spiza*
Blue dacnis	*Dacnis cayana*
Golden-rumped euphonia	*Euphonia cyanocephala*
Trinidad euphonia	*Euphonia trinitatis*
Violaceous euphonia	*Euphonia violocea*
Speckled tanager	*Tangara guttata*
Turquoise tanager	*Tangara mexicana*

Bay-headed tanager	*Tangara gyrola*
Blue-gray tanager	*Thraupis episcopus*
Palm tanager	*Thraupis palmarum*
Blue-capped tanager	*Thraupis cyanocephala*
Silver-beaked tanager	*Ramphocelus carbo*
Hepatic tanager	*Piranga flava*
Summer tanager	*Piranga rubra*
Scarlet tanager	*Piranga olivacea*
Red-crowned ant-tanager	*Habia rubica*
White-lined tanager	*Tachyphonus rufus*
White-shouldered tanager	*Tachyphonus luctuosus*

GROSBEAKS & BUNTINGS

Grayish saltator	*Saltator coerulescens*
Streaked saltator	*Saltator albicollis*
Red-capped cardinal	*Paroaria gularis*
Rose-breasted grosbeak	*Pheucticus ludovicianus*
Dickcissel	*Spiza americana*
Indigo bunting	*Passerina cyanea*
Blue-black grassquit	*Volatinia jacarina*
Black-faced grassquit	*Tiaris bicolor*
Sooty grassquit	*Tiaris fuliginosa*
Slate-colored seedeater	*Sporophila schistacea*
Gray seedeater	*Sporophila intermedia*
Variable seedeater	*Sporophila americana*
Lesson's seedeater	*Sporophila bouvronides*
Yellow-bellied seedeater	*Sporophila nigricollis*
Ruddy-breasted seedeater	*Sporophila minuta*
Large-billed seed-finch	*Oryzoborus crassirostris*
Lesser seed-finch	*Oryzoborus angolensis*
Orange-fronted yellow-finch	*Sicalis columbiana*
Saffron finch	*Sicalis flaveola*

FINCHES

Red siskin	*Spinus cucullata*

SEASONAL DISTRIBUTION OF THE BIRDS
OF TRINIDAD AND TOBAGO

The following section provides a quick means of determining the likelihood of sighting a particular species of bird at a specific time of year. No attempt has been made in this section to distinguish between relative abundances in Trinidad and in Tobago. Whatever information is available on that topic is contained in the section entitled "Target Species in Trinidad and Tobago." The chance of finding a particular species is based on the assumption that the birder investigates proper habitat during the proper season and exercises due caution, avoiding loud noises, sudden movements, flashy clothing, and behavior inappropriate to the quest.

KEY

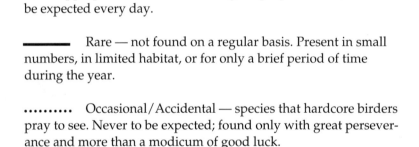

Common — almost certain to be found every day in appropriate habitat and during the proper season.

Uncommon — possible to find with diligent searching in the appropriate habitat and during the proper season, but not to be expected every day.

Rare — not found on a regular basis. Present in small numbers, in limited habitat, or for only a brief period of time during the year.

Occasional/Accidental — species that hardcore birders pray to see. Never to be expected; found only with great perseverance and more than a modicum of good luck.

Little tinamou
Least grebe
Pied-billed grebe
Audubon's shearwater
Leach's storm-petrel
Red-billed tropicbird
Brown booby
Red-footed booby
Brown pelican
Neotropic cormorant
Anhinga
Magnificent frigatebird
Pinnated bittern
Stripe-backed bittern
Least bittern
Rufescent tiger-heron
Great blue heron
Cocoi heron
Great egret
Little egret
Western reef-heron
Snowy egret
Little blue heron
Tricolored heron
Cattle egret
Green (incl. striated) heron
Black-crowned night-heron
Yellow-crowned night-heron
Boat-billed heron
Scarlet ibis

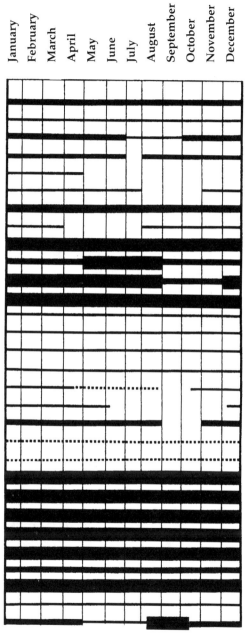

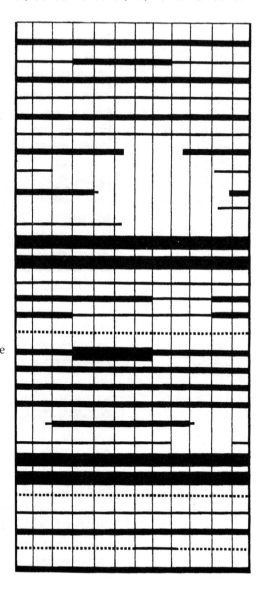

	January	February	March	April	May	June	July	August	September	October	November	December
Glossy ibis												
Roseate spoonbill												
Fulvous whistling-duck												
White-faced whistling-duck												
Black-bellied whistling-duck												
White-cheeked pintail												
Blue-winged teal												
Northern shoveler												
American wigeon												
Lesser scaup												
Masked duck												
Black vulture												
Turkey vulture												
King vulture												
Osprey												
Gray-headed kite												
Hook-billed kite												
American swallow-tailed kite												
Pearl kite												
White-tailed kite												
Double-toothed kite												
Plumbeous kite												
Long-winged harrier												
White hawk												
Common black-hawk												
Rufous crab-hawk												
Great black-hawk												
Savanna hawk												
Black-collared hawk												
Gray hawk												

	January	February	March	April	May	June	July	August	September	October	November	December

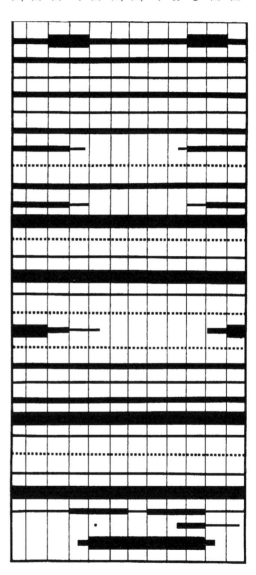

Broad-winged hawk
Short-tailed hawk
White-tailed hawk
Zone-tailed hawk
Ornate hawk-eagle
Yellow-headed caracara
Merlin
Aplomado falcon
Bat falcon
Peregrine falcon
Rufous-vented chachalaca
Common piping-guan
Gray-breasted crake
Clapper rail
Gray-necked wood-rail
Rufous-necked wood-rail
Sora
Ash-throated crake
Yellow-breasted crake
Spotted rail
Purple gallinule
Common moorhen
Caribbean coot
Sungrebe
Limpkin
Southern lapwing
Black-bellied plover
Lesser golden-plover
Collared plover
Wilson's plover

145

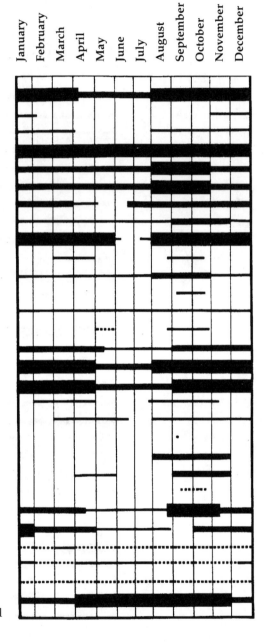

	January	February	March	April	May	June	July	August	September	October	November	December
Semipalmated plover												
Killdeer												
Black-necked stilt												
Wattled jacana												
Greater yellowlegs												
Lesser yellowlegs												
Solitary sandpiper												
Willet												
Spotted sandpiper												
Upland sandpiper												
Whimbrel												
Hudsonian godwit												
Ruddy turnstone												
Red knot												
Sanderling												
Semipalmated sandpiper												
Western sandpiper												
Least sandpiper												
White-rumped sandpiper												
Baird's sandpiper												
Pectoral sandpiper												
Stilt sandpiper												
Buff-breasted sandpiper												
Short-billed dowitcher												
Common snipe												
Pomarine jaeger												
Parasitic jaeger												
South Polar skua												
Laughing gull												
Common black-headed gull												

	January	February	March	April	May	June	July	August	September	October	November	December

Ring-billed gull
Herring gull
Gull-billed tern
Royal tern
Sandwich tern
Roseate tern
Common tern
Least tern
Yellow-billed tern
Bridled tern
Sooty tern
Large-billed tern
Black tern
Brown noddy
Black skimmer
Rock dove
Pale-vented pigeon
Scaled pigeon
Band-tailed pigeon
Eared dove
Scaled dove
Common ground-dove
Plain-breasted ground-dove
Ruddy ground-dove
Blue ground-dove
White-tipped dove
Gray-fronted dove
Ruddy quail-dove
Lined quail-dove
Red-bellied macaw

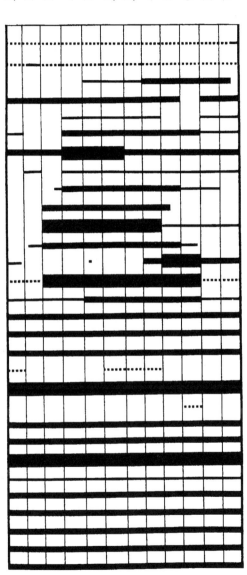

Green-rumped parrotlet
Lilac-tailed parrotlet
Blue-headed parrot
Orange-winged parrot
Yellow-billed cuckoo
Mangrove cuckoo
Squirrel cuckoo
Little cuckoo
Striped cuckoo
Greater ani
Smooth-billed ani
Common barn-owl
Tropical screech-owl
Spectacled owl
Ferruginous pygmy-owl
Mottled owl
Striped owl
Short-tailed nighthawk
Lesser nighthawk
Nacunda nighthawk
Common pauraque
Rufous nightjar
White-tailed nightjar
Common potoo
Oilbird
Chestnut-collared swift
White-collared swift
Chapman's swift
Short-tailed swift
Band-rumped swift

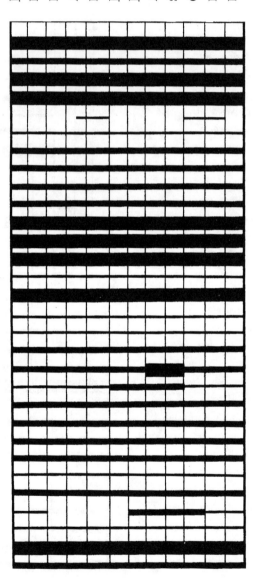

Gray-rumped swift
Lesser swallow-tailed swift
Fork-tailed palm-swift
Rufous-breasted hermit
Green hermit
Little hermit
White-tailed sabrewing
White-necked jacobin
Brown violet-ear
Green-throated mango
Black-throated mango
Ruby-topaz hummingbird
Tufted coquette
Blue-chinned sapphire
Blue-tailed emerald
White-chested emerald
White-tailed goldenthroat
Copper-rumped hummingbird
Long-billed starthroat
White-tailed trogon
Violaceous trogon
Collared trogon
Blue-crowned motmot
Ringed kingfisher
Belted kingfisher
Green kingfisher
American pygmy-kingfisher
Rufous-tailed jacamar
Channel-billed toucan
Red-crowned woodpecker

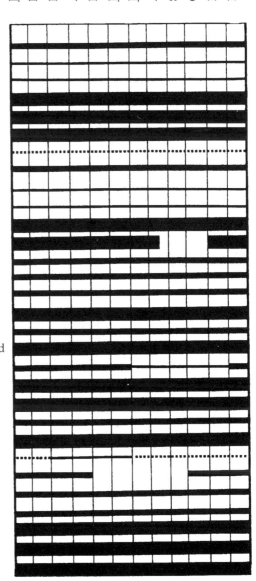

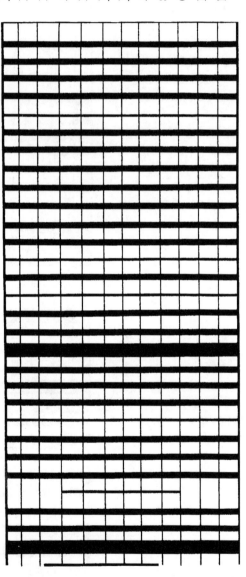

	January	February	March	April	May	June	July	August	September	October	November	December
Red-rumped woodpecker												
Golden-olive woodpecker												
Chestnut woodpecker												
Lineated woodpecker												
Crimson-crested woodpecker												
Pale-breasted spinetail												
Stripe-breasted spinetail												
Yellow-chinned spinetail												
Streaked xenops												
Gray-throated leaftosser												
Plain-brown woodcreeper												
Olivaceous woodcreeper												
Straight-billed woodcreeper												
Buff-throated woodcreeper												
Streak-headed woodcreeper												
Great antshrike												
Black-crested antshrike												
Barred antshrike												
Plain antvireo												
White-flanked antwren												
White-fringed antwren												
Silvered antbird												
White-bellied antbird												
Black-faced antthrush												
Southern beardless-tyrannulet												
Mouse-colored tyrannulet												
Scrub flycatcher												
Forest elaenia												
Yellow-bellied elaenia												
Lesser elaenia												

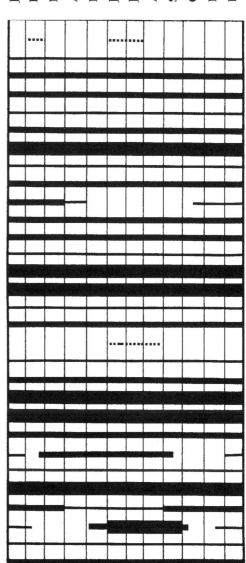

	January	February	March	April	May	June	July	August	September	October	November	December
Crested doradito		••••				•••••	•••••					
Olive-striped flycatcher												
Ochre-bellied flycatcher												
Slaty-capped flycatcher												
Short-tailed pygmy-tyrant												
Yellow-olive flycatcher												
Yellow-breasted flycatcher												
White-throated spadebill												
Bran-colored flycatcher												
Olive-sided flycatcher												
Tropical pewee												
Euler's flycatcher												
Fuscous flycatcher												
Pied water-tyrant												
White-head. marsh-tyrant												
Bright-rumped attila												
Dusky-capped flycatcher												
Swainson's flycatcher						•• ■	•••••••••					
Venezuelan flycatcher												
Brown-crested flycatcher												
Great kiskadee												
Boat-billed flycatcher												
Streaked flycatcher												
Piratic flycatcher												
Sulphury flycatcher												
Tropical kingbird												
Gray kingbird												
Fork-tailed flycatcher												
White-winged becard												
Black-tailed tityra												

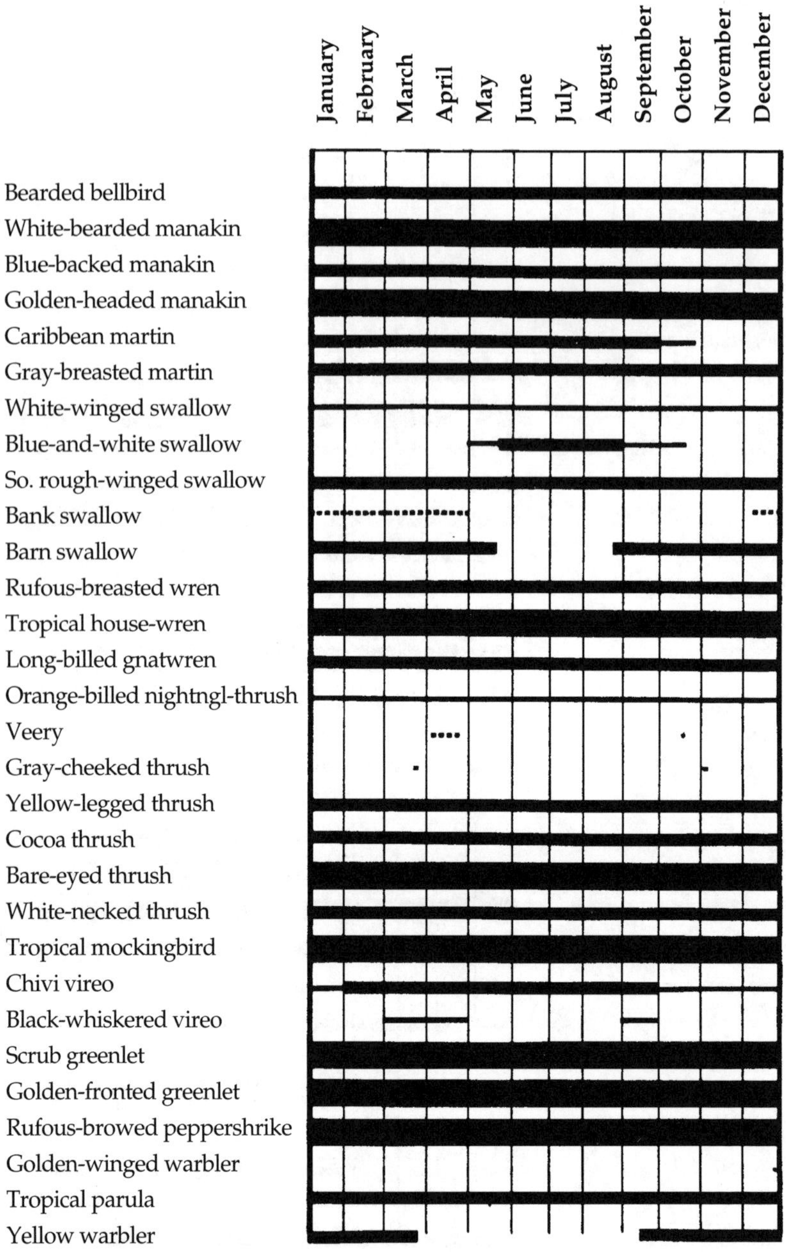

	January	February	March	April	May	June	July	August	September	October	November	December

Bearded bellbird
White-bearded manakin
Blue-backed manakin
Golden-headed manakin
Caribbean martin
Gray-breasted martin
White-winged swallow
Blue-and-white swallow
So. rough-winged swallow
Bank swallow
Barn swallow
Rufous-breasted wren
Tropical house-wren
Long-billed gnatwren
Orange-billed nightngl-thrush
Veery
Gray-cheeked thrush
Yellow-legged thrush
Cocoa thrush
Bare-eyed thrush
White-necked thrush
Tropical mockingbird
Chivi vireo
Black-whiskered vireo
Scrub greenlet
Golden-fronted greenlet
Rufous-browed peppershrike
Golden-winged warbler
Tropical parula
Yellow warbler

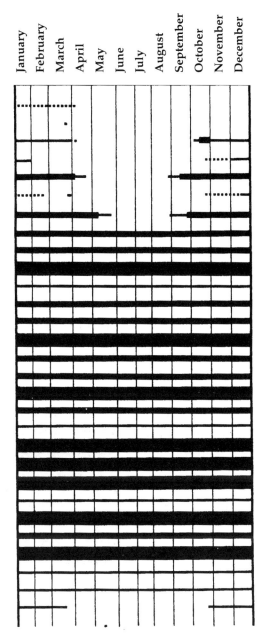

Cape May warbler
Prairie warbler
Blackpoll warbler
Black-and-white warbler
American redstart
Prothonotary warbler
Northern waterthrush
Masked yellowthroat
Golden-crowned warbler
Bananaquit
Bicolored conebill
Speckled tanager
Turquoise tanager
Bay-headed tanager
Blue dacnis
Green honeycreeper
Purple honeycreeper
Red-legged honeycreeper
Trinidad euphonia
Violaceous euphonia
Blue-gray tanager
Palm tanager
Blue-capped tanager
Silver-beaked tanager
White-shouldered tanager
White-lined tanager
Red-crowned ant-tanager
Hepatic tanager
Summer tanager
Scarlet tanager

	January	February	March	April	May	June	July	August	September	October	November	December
Swallow-Tanager												
Streaked saltator												
Grayish saltator												
Red-capped cardinal												
Indigo bunting												
Dickcissel												
Blue-black grassquit												
Variable seedeater												
Lesson's seedeater												
Yellow-bellied seedeater												
Ruddy-breasted seedeater												
Lesser seed-finch												
Black-faced grassquit												
Sooty grassquit												
Saffron finch												
Bobolink												
Red-winged blackbird												
Red-breasted blackbird												
Yellow-hooded blackbird												
Carib grackle												
Shiny cowbird												
Giant cowbird												
Moriche oriole												
Yellow oriole												
Yellow-rumped cacique												
Crested oropendola												

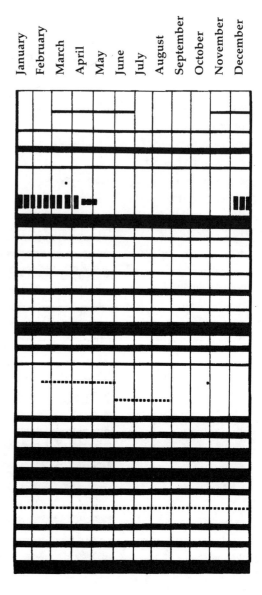

INDEX

155

157